Rocky Mountain Flower Finder

by Janet L. Wingate, Ph.D.

a guide to wildflowers found below tree line in the Rocky Mountains

illustrations by the author

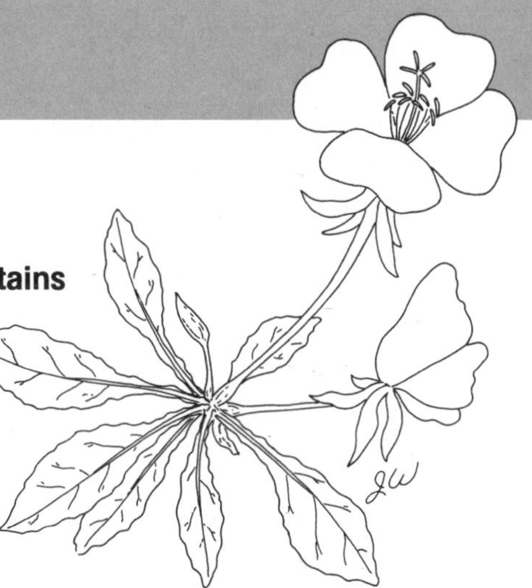

Nature Study Guild, Berkeley, California

To use this book

find some typical flowers and leaves of the plant you want to identify, then turn to the key on page 6, make the first choice, and go on from there. (There's a simpler key for tiny flowers on page 4.)

Advice:

A 10X hand lens will help you see small flower parts.

The first three pages explain terms and give useful information.

Plant families appear in alphabetical order of their Latin names.

This book is about herbaceous wildflowers of six U.S. Rocky Mountain states, including the foothill, montane and subalpine zones as defined on page 3.

Cover by Erica Watts.

area covered by this book

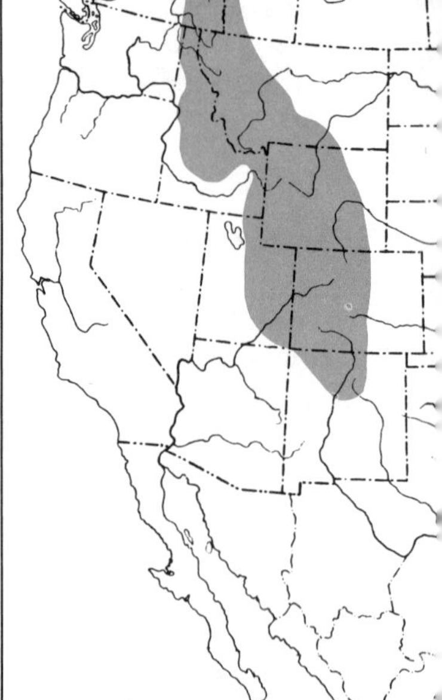

Glossary—terms that describe flowers

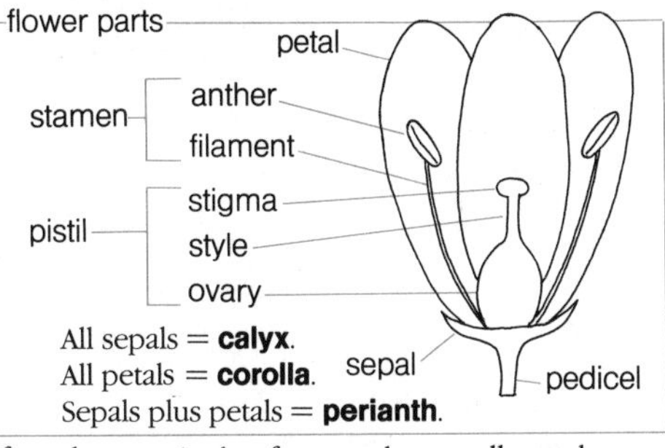
flower parts
petal
stamen
anther
filament
pistil
stigma
style
ovary
sepal
pedicel

All sepals = **calyx**.
All petals = **corolla**.
Sepals plus petals = **perianth**.

If petals are united to form a tube, corolla can be removed from flower in one piece. If petals are separate, you can remove them one at a time.

Flowers having all petals alike are called **regular**.

Flowers with petals of different shapes and sizes are **irregular.**

Ovaries above petals and sepals are **superior**.

Those below are **inferior**.

Some flowers have a slender, sac-like projection called a **spur**.

Flowers may have leaf-like appendages called **bracts**.

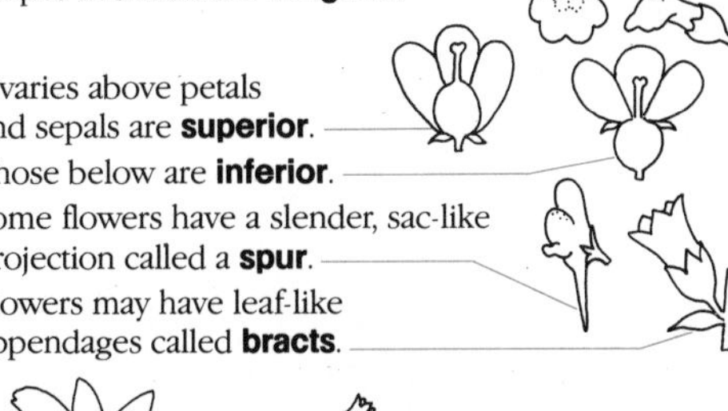

Flowers may be alone, solitary, or grouped into one of the following kinds of infloresence:

- crowded tightly together, unstalked, in a **head**
  (Usually with bracts under the head.)
- along a stem, with stalks, in a **raceme**
- along a stem, unstalked, in a **spike**
- in a branched arrangement, a **panicle**
- clustered with all stalks arising from one point, an **umbel**
  (An umbellet is an umbel within an umbel.)

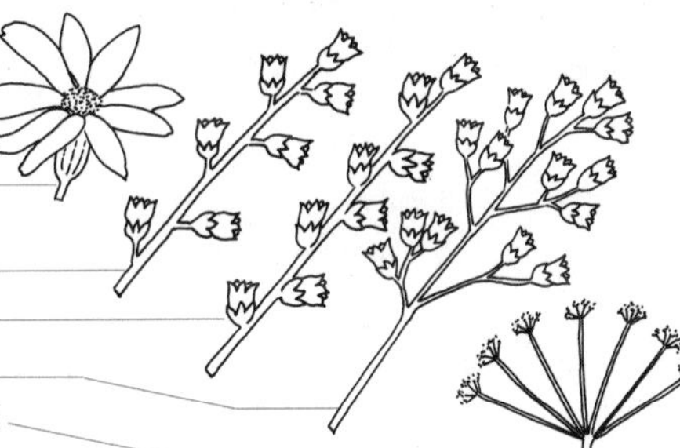

② Glossary—terms that describe leaves

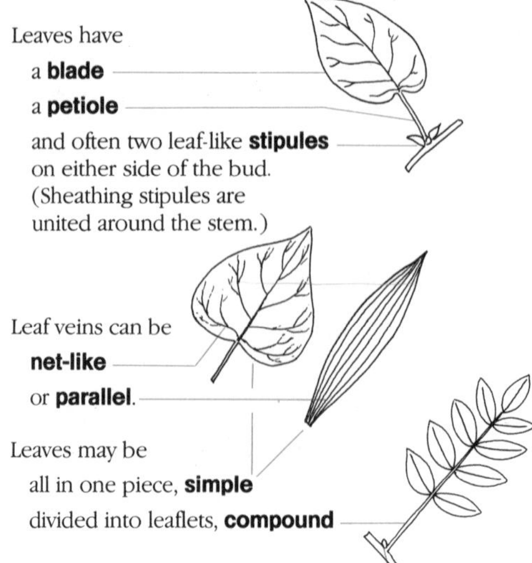

Leaves have

a **blade**

a **petiole**

and often two leaf-like **stipules** on either side of the bud. (Sheathing stipules are united around the stem.)

Leaf veins can be

net-like

or **parallel**.

Leaves may be

all in one piece, **simple**

divided into leaflets, **compound**

(You can tell a leaf from a leaflet by the bud. Buds are found at the base of the whole leaf, but are never at a leaflet base.)

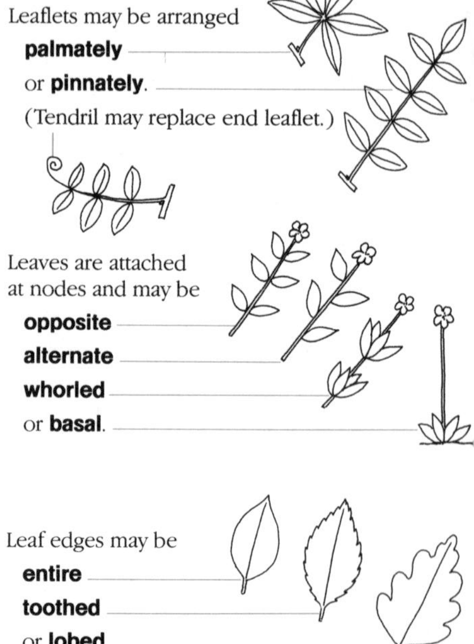

Leaflets may be arranged

palmately

or **pinnately**.

(Tendril may replace end leaflet.)

Leaves are attached at nodes and may be

opposite

alternate

whorled

or **basal**.

Leaf edges may be

entire

toothed

or **lobed**.

Habitats

Here are abbreviations used for each plant's habitat:

wet mdws, aspn = in wet meadows, aspen groves
dry, rky slps = on dry, rocky slopes
opn, grvl mdws = in open gravelly meadows
mst wds, thkts = in moist woods, thickets
rdsds, dist soil = on roadsides, in disturbed soil
intro = introduced species

Ranges

Dots show in which of the six Rocky Mountain states each species is found (but it may also occur in states or areas not shown on the map). Plants confined to one side of the continental divide will have an E or W next to the map. Plants found mostly east or west of the divide, or mostly in the northern or southern part of the range shown here, will be designated as ME, MW, MN, MS.

W

ME

Life Zones

The Rocky Mountain life zone (s) for each plant are shown by initial letters in bold type:

A **Alpine Zone**—The highest-elevation zone is above tree line. (Plants found only here are not included in this book.)

S **Subalpine Zone**—Spring comes late to lush meadows and bogs, with engelmann spruce, subalpine fir, and often aspen. Limber, whitebark, or bristlecone pine may occupy ridges.

M **Montane Zone**—Meadows are warmer and dryer, with douglas fir, aspen, and lodgepole pine; ponderosa pine on warm slopes; white fir or blue spruce in canyons, along streams.

F **Foothill Zone**—Spring comes earliest, meadows may be dry by July. Ponderosa pine gives way to grass, sagebrush and shrubs at lower elevations.

P **Plains Zone**—Low elevation non-mountainous areas (not included in this book).

The life zones are at lower altitudes to the north, higher in the south. The subalpine zone begins at about 10,000 ft. in southern Colorado and 8,000 ft. in Montana. And the zones are higher on sunny south-facing slopes than on cooler north-facing slopes. But the trees will tell you what zone you're in.

Key to Tiny Flowers—Use this key only if the whole flower is small enough to fit into this circle: 

Choose the leaf type, then read down the list 'til you find a match.

Leaves alternate and simple

- Flowers in heads — **Sunflower Family** p27
- Flowers irregular — **Orchid Family** p91
- Sheathing stipules — **Buckwheat Family** p97
- Petals absent, sepals petal-like — **Sandalwood Family** p112
- Petals four, ovary inferior — **Evening Primrose Family** p88
- Petals four; ovary superior — **Mustard Family** p51
- Petals five, united — **Borage Family** p48
- Petals appear to be six; leaves parallel veined — **Lily Family** p79

Leaves alternate and compound

- Petals four; fruit below flowers — **Mustard Family** p51
- Flowers in umbels — **Parsley Family** p20
- Leaflets three; flowers irregular — **Pea Family** p67
- Flower looks like this — **Phlox Family** p94
- Flowers in heads — **Sunflower Family** p27

Leaves whorled

- Umbels — **Buckwheat Family** p97
- Stem square — **Madder Family** p112

(tiny flowers continued)

Leaves opposite and simple	Juice milky	**Dogbane Family** p26
	Flowers blue or yellow	**Figwort Family** p115
	Stem square	**Mint Family** p76
	Flowers irregular with lip	**Orchid Family** p91
	Nodes often enlarged; leaves entire	**Pink Family** p62
	Stems reclining	**Verbena Family** p119
	Petals four	**Evening Primrose Family** p88
Leaves opposite and compound	Stems erect	**Valerian Family** p119
	Stems reclining	**Verbena Family** p119
Leaves entirely basal and simple	Petals three	**Arrowhead Family** p19
	Leaves parallel-veined	**Lily Family** p79
	Umbels, leaf undersides wooly	**Buckwheat Family** p97
	Umbels, leaf undersides not wooly	**Primrose Family** p100
	Not as above	**Saxifrage Family** p113
Leaves entirely basal and compound	Leaflets three; flowers not in umbels	**Rose Family** p108
	Leaflets oval, finely toothed; umbels	**Ginseng Family** p26
	Leaflets not as above; umbels	**Parsley Family** p20

(A few tiny wildflowers are not included in the above key, so if you don't find a match, try p6.)

BEGIN HERE—Key to Wildflower Families

If plant lacks chlorophyll (not green), see Group 1 below.

If plant is green, and has many small stemless flowers, in a head which looks like a single flower; ovary inferior, see — **Sunflower Family** p27

If flowers are unlike the above, and are

- regular, with petals that are
  - separate — **Group 2** p7
  - united — **Group 3** p13
- irregular — **Group 4** p17

Group 1—plants without chlorophyll

Flowers regular — **Wintergreen Family** p101

Flowers irregular, with petals

- separate — **Orchid Family** p91
- united — **Broomrape Family** p93

Group 2—plants with regular flowers, petals separate

Stamens few (ten or less, or hard-to-see) —— next page

Stamens too many to count, easy to see; petals number

- three —— **Arrowhead Family** p19
- more than three; leaves are
  - large, floating on water —— **Waterlily Family** p87
  - rough like sandpaper —— **Stick-leaf Family** p85
  - opposite with translucent dots —— **St. Johnswort Family** p75
  - spiny —— **Poppy Family** p93
  - absent —— **Cactus Family** p58
  - not as above; filaments are
    - united into a tube —— **Mallow Family** p86
    - not united; sepals
      - appear united at base —— **Rose Family** p108
      - are separate at base, (sepals may be petal-like); flowers
        - have 12-18 pink petals —— **Purslane Family** p99
        - not as above —— **Buttercup Family** p103

stamens

8 (from p7)

The number of petals (and similar petal-like sepals, if any) is

- four — next page
- five — p10
- three, and flowers are
  - bright blue to magenta — **Spiderwort Family** p65
  - white to pale lavender or blue tinged, with stem leaves
    - absent — **Arrowhead Family** p19
    - present — **Lily Family** p79
- six (sepals petal-like), and they're
  - blue, with flowers
    - several in a raceme; ovary superior — **Lily Family** p79
    - fewer; ovary inferior — **Iris Family** p75
  - not blue; leaves are
    - woolly hairy on underside or shaped like this: — **Buckwheat Family** p97
    - stiff, spine-tipped — **Agave Family** p19
    - large and pleated, or not as above — **Lily Family** p79
- six to eight (sepals not petal-like) — **Purslane Family** p99

(from p8)

Petals are absent; sepals are petal-like, white, greenish or pinkish — **Sandalwood Family** p112

Petals are present; leaves are

- opposite or whorled; stamens number
  - four; ovary superior — **Gentian Family** p70
  - eight; ovary inferior — **Evening Primrose Family** p88
- alternate or basal, and are
  - palmately compound — **Caper Family** p61
  - pinnately compound or simple; flower has
    - four pistils — **Stonecrop Family** p66
    - one pistil, and stamens number
      - six; ovary superior — **Mustard Family** p51
      - eight; ovary inferior — **Evening Primrose Family** p88

10

(from p8)

Flowers nodding, may turn up as they fade —— **Wintergreen Family** p101

Flowers not as above; leaves are

- alternate or basal —— next page
- opposite or whorled; plant juice is
  - milky —— **Milkweed Family** p26
  - not milky; flower has
    - two sepals, easily seen —— **Purslane Family** p99
    - five sepals; leaves are
      - lobed or compound —— **Geranium Family** p73
      - not as above; petals are
        - pure white (sometimes pink or red); ten stamens —— **Pink Family** p62
        - rarely pure white (sometimes tinged with green or blue); five stamens —— **Gentian Family** p70

Leaves simple (may be deeply lobed); stem

- is leafless; basal leaves are
  - palmately veined — **Saxifrage Family** p113
  - not palmately veined; flowers are
    - pointed like a dart — **Primrose Family** p100
    - not as above, — **Saxifrage Family** p113
- has well developed leaves (at least one) — next page

Leaves compound with three heart-shaped leaflets; flowers yellow — **Wood Sorrel Family** p93

Leaves compound, but not as above; fruit is

- like a stork's beak; flowers pink — **Geranium Family** p73
- not as above; flowers are
  - in umbels; leaves are
    - basal with finely toothed, oval leaflets — **Ginseng Family** p26
    - not as above — **Parsley Family** p20
  - not in umbels; petals
    - cleft into 3-5 segments — **Saxifrage Family** p113
    - not cleft — **Rose Family** p108

(12) (from p11)

Flowers are blue or dull purple; leaves are

- mostly basal — **Gentian Family** p70
- not as above — **Flax Family** p85

Flowers not as above; stipules

- sheathing; flowers in a spike — **Buckwheat Family** p97
- not as above; petals are
  - absent, sepals petal-like, white, greenish or pinkish — **Sandalwood Family** p112
  - present; fruit is
    - long-beaked; stem usually branched — **Geranium Family** p73
    - not as above; sepals number
      - two, easily seen — **Purslane Family** p99
      - five, leaves are
        - fleshy; pistils five — **Stonecrop Family** p66
        - not as above — **Saxifrage Family** p113

Group 3—plants with regular flowers, petals united (from p6)

Leaves alternate or entirely basal —— p15

Leaves whorled (or appear so); flowers are

- white, tiny; stem square —— **Madder Family** p112
- yellow to pale-yellow or cream; underside of leaf is
  - woolly-hairy —— **Buckwheat Family** p97
  - not as above —— **Phlox Family** p94

Leaves opposite (at least lower ones); flowers are

- bright red —— **Evening Primrose Family** p88
- not as above; all flowers are
  - in pairs, nodding —— **Honeysuckle Family** p61
  - not as above, juice is
    - milky; flowers are
      - in umbels —— **Milkweed Family** p26
      - not in umbels —— **Dogbane Family** p26
    - not milky —— next page

14 (from p13)

Leaves pinnately compound or deeply lobed; stem is

- erect — **Valerian Family** p119
- reclining — **Verbena Family** p119

Leaves not as above; bracts below flowers are

- united into a cup or saucer — **Four-o'clock Family** p87
- not as above, or absent; flowers are
  - tiny, blue, in a raceme; stamens two — **Figwort Family** p115
  - shaped like this
    style three-branched — **Phlox Family** p94
  - shaped differently — **Gentian Family** p70

(from p13)

Plant is trailing vine with arrowhead shaped leaves — **Morning Glory Family** p65

Plant not as above; petals number

- three plus three similar petal-like sepals; flowers are
  - blue, arranged
    - in umbel — **Lily Family** p79
    - not in umbel — **Iris Family** p75
  - not blue; leaves are
    - woolly-hairy on under surface — **Buckwheat Family** p97
    - not as above — **Lily Family** p79
- four or five; flowers are
  - yellow on fuzzy 2-5ft spike — **Figwort Family** p115
  - not as above; flowers are
    - pointed like a dart — **Primrose Family** p100
    - not as above; stamens are
      - longer than petals, extending beyond them (exserted); flowers are
        - in clusters, often coiled — **Waterleaf Family** p74
        - in open panicle — **Phlox Family** p94
      - shorter — next page

 (from p15)

- Stem leaves absent — **Primrose Family** p100
- Stem leaves present; stamens are
  - many and united into a tube — **Mallow Family** p86
  - not as above; leaves are
    - compound — **Phlox Family** p94
    - simple; petals are
      - absent, sepals petal-like, white, greenish or pinkish — **Sandalwood Family** p112
      - present; ovary is
        - inferior — **Bellflower Family** p60
        - superior, four-lobed — **Borage Family** p48
        - superior, not four-lobed — **Phlox Family** p94

Group 4—plants with irregular flowers

(from p6)

Leaves all simple, entire or toothed —— next page

Leaves (at least some) compound or deeply lobed; plant is
- aquatic (or in mud of drying pond) —— **Bladderwort Family** p79
- not aquatic; leaves are
  - opposite; stem is
    - erect —— **Valerian Family** p119
    - reclining —— **Verbena Family** p119
  - alternate; flower is
    - shaped like elephant head —— **Figwort Family** p115
    - not as above; spur is
      - present; flowers are
        - yellow or pink; stamens six —— **Fumitory Family** p70
        - blue to purple; stamens many —— **Buttercup Family** p103
      - absent; flowers are
        - hooded —— **Buttercup Family** p103
        - pea like —— **Pea Family** p67
        - not as above —— **Figwort Family** p115

hood

(18) (from p17)

Leaves alternate, basal, or opposite with only two leaves; flowers

- resemble garden violets — **Violet Family** p119
- have lip or sac-like lower petal — **Orchid Family** p91
- not as above — **Figwort Family** p115

Leaves opposite with several leaves; stem cross section is

- round — **Figwort Family** p115
- square; flowers are
  - brownish, greenish, red, or yellow; ovary not four-lobed — **Figwort Family** p115
  - white, pink, purplish, lavender, or blue; ovary four-lobed — **Mint Family** p76

AGAVE FAMILY *(Agavaceae)* Xerophytic plants with narrow, stiff, spine-tipped leaves. Flowers regular, white or cream-colored with three petals, three petal-like sepals. Stamens six, ovary superior.

Spanish Bayonet
Yucca glauca
Y. baccata (Banana Yucca), wide leaves;
Y. harrimaniae, narrow leaves, W of Divide.

ARROWHEAD FAMILY *(Alismataceae)* Aquatic or marsh herbs. Flowers regular with three separate white petals, three greenish sepals, six to many stamens, many pistils. Leaves basal.

Leaves arrowhead shaped,
Arrowhead
Sagittaria cuneata
S. latifolia, low elevations.

Leaves not as above,
Water Plantain
Alisma plantago-aquatica

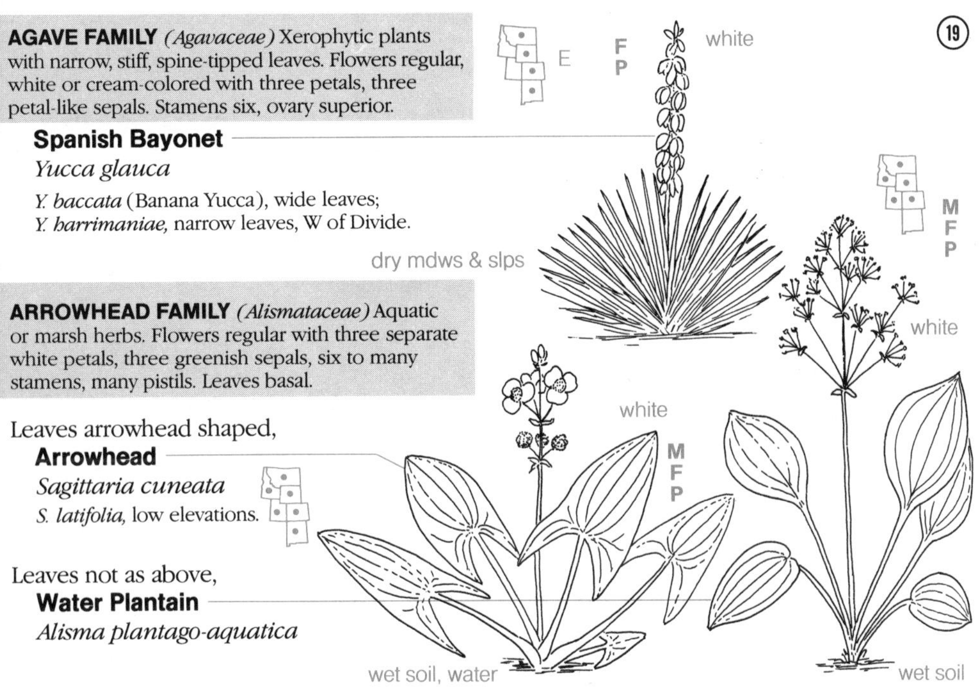
E
F
P
white
dry mdws & slps
M
F
P
white
white
M
F
P
wet soil, water
wet soil

PARSLEY or CARROT FAMILY *(Apiaceae or Umbelliferae)* Herbs with tiny regular flowers in umbels. Flower parts in fives, petals separate, ovary inferior. Leaves usually compound. Includes very poisonous as well as edible plants.

Flowers not yellow, p22.

Flowers yellow; leaflet segments are

- very narrow, next page.
- wider; leaflets are
  - minutely spine-tipped, **Mountain Caraway** *Aletes acaulis*
  - not as above, **Musineon** *Musineon divaricatum*

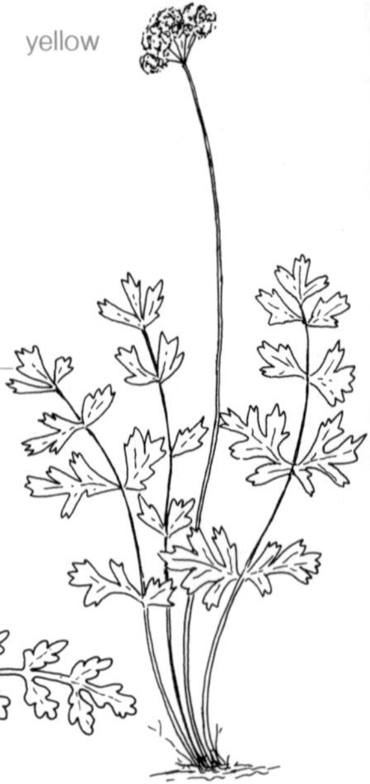

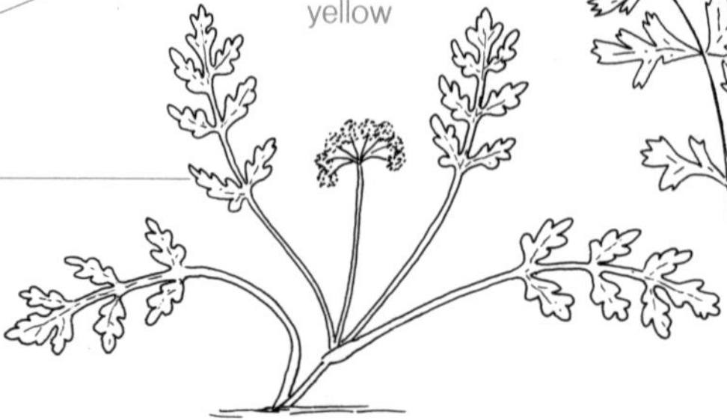

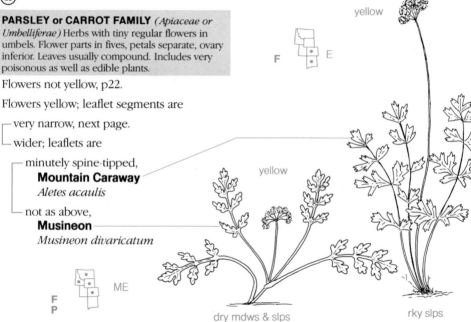

yellow

F E

rky slps

yellow

F P ME

dry mdws & slps

Parsley (from p20)

- Plant robust, 1-4ft tall,
  - **Indian Balsam** *Lomatium dissectum*
- Plant slender, with leaf segments
  - less than ¼ in long,
    - **Milfoil Biscuitroot** *Lomatium grayi*
  - longer, and segments
    - often over 1/16 in wide and gradually tapering to a point,
      - **Mountain Parsley** *Pseudocymopterus montanus*
    - narrower, not tapering to a point,
      - **Whiskbroom Parsley** *Harbouria trachypleura*

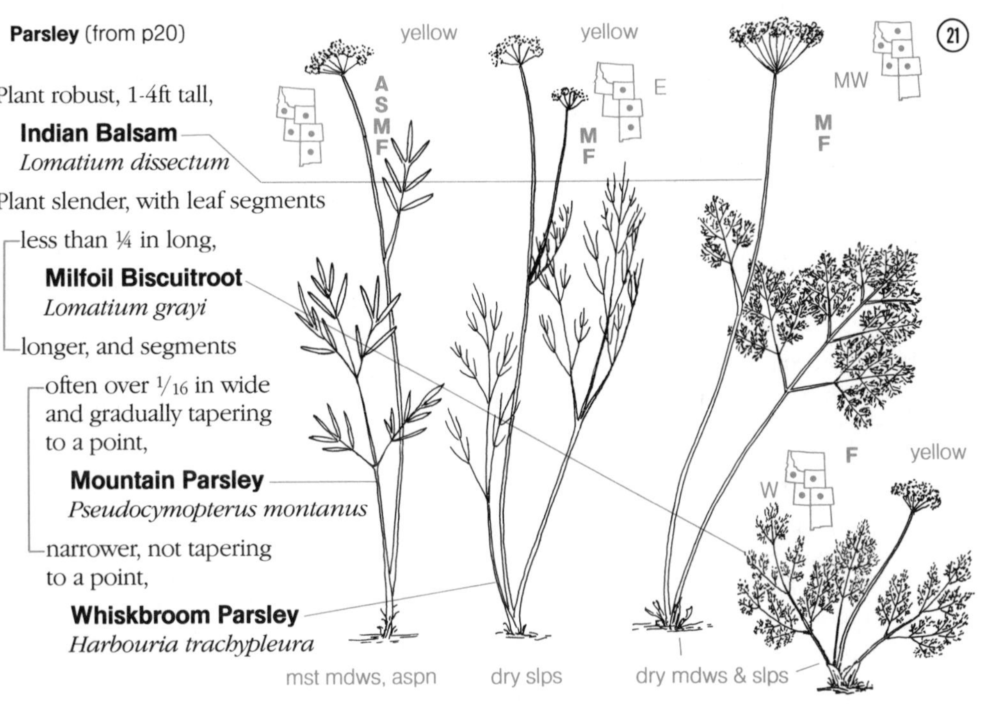
yellow
ASMF
mst mdws, aspn
yellow
E
MF
dry slps
MW
MF
dry mdws & slps
F
yellow
W

(22) **Parsley** (from p20)

Leaves more than once compound (leaflets divided into additional leaflets), next page.

Leaves once compound (leaflets undivided); leaflets number

- three; plant large,
  Cow Parsnip
  Heracleum sphondylium ssp. *montanum*
- more than three; leaves are
  - palmately compound,
    Snakeroot
    Sanicula marilandica
  - pinnately compound; leaflets of lower leaves are
    - very narrow,
      Yampa
      Perideridia gairdneri
    - wider,
      Cowbane
      Oxypolis fendleri

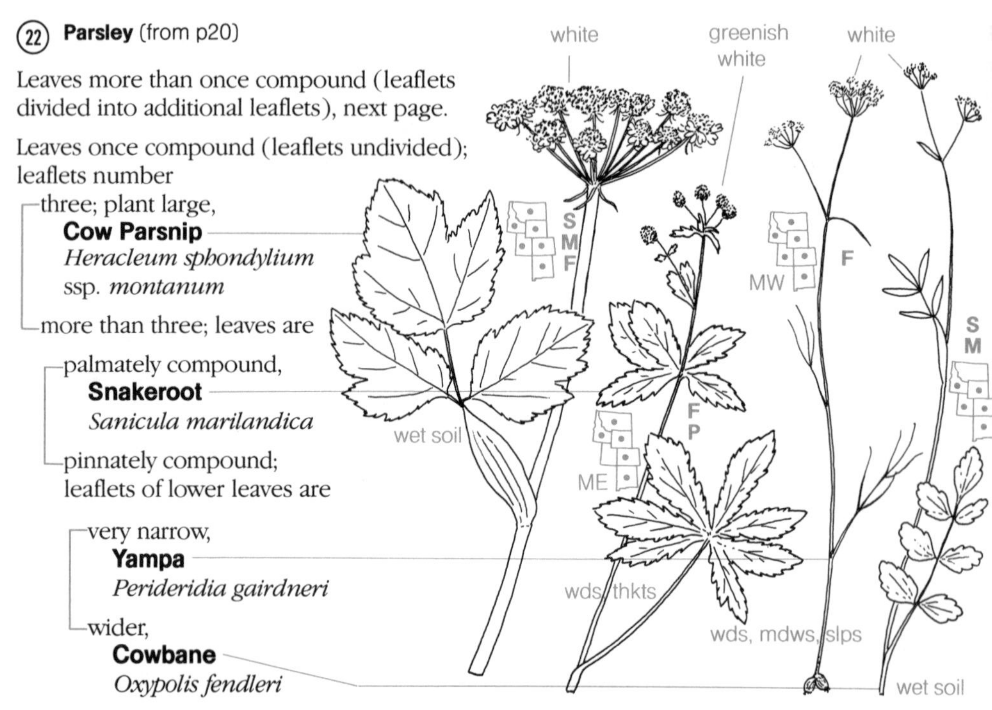

white
greenish white
white
S M F
wet soil
MW
F
F P
ME
wds, thkts
wds, mdws, slps
S M
wet soil

Parsley (from p22)

Plant a small spring-flowering perennial with grayish leaves,

Salt-and-pepper
Lomatium orientale

Plant not as above; flowers or fruits number

- five or fewer per umbellet; fruit club-shaped,
  Sweet Cicely
  Osmorhiza depauperata
- more than five; stem is
  - purple-spotted,
    Poison Hemlock
    Conium maculatum
    (poisonous)
  - not purple-spotted, next page.

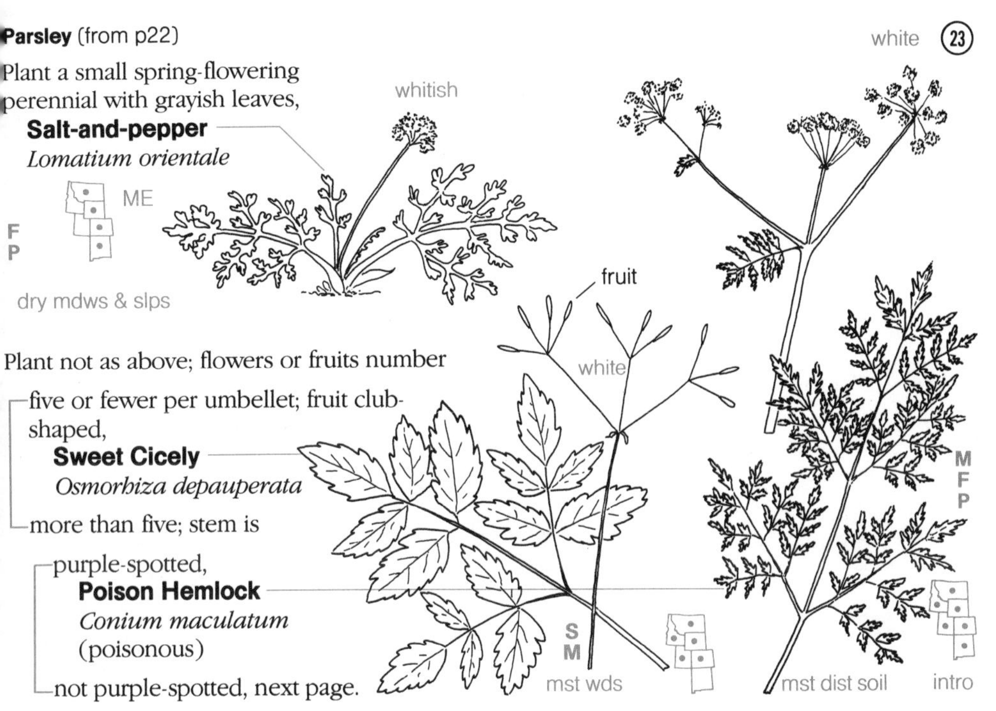
whitish
ME
F
P
dry mdws & slps
fruit
white
S
M
mst wds
white
M
F
P
mst dist soil
intro

Parsley (from p23)

Main veins of leaflets end in notches,
Water Hemlock
Cicuta douglasii
(poisonous)

Main veins end at tips of teeth; leaflets are

- not finely divided, next page.
- finely divided into segments about 1/32 in. wide; leaflet segments of lower or basal leaves are
  - sessile, clasping main leaf stem,
    Caraway
    Carum carvi
  - stalked,
    Fern-leaved Lovage
    Ligusticum tenuifolium

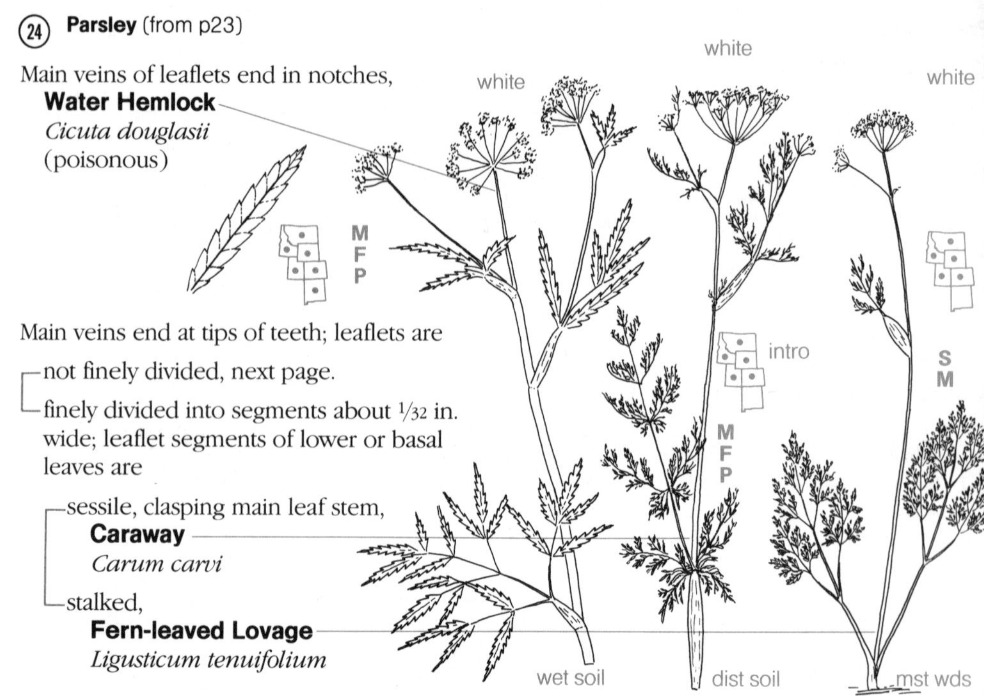
white
white
white
M
F
P
intro
M
F
P
S
M
wet soil
dist soil
mst wds

Parsley (from p24)

Umbels round; plant is

– over 3ft tall,
Giant Angelica
Angelica ampla

– under 2ft tall, Grays Angelica, below

Umbels not round; stem is

– short, thick; flowers brownish purple,
Grays Angelica
Angelica grayi
A. roseana (Rose Angelica), flowers white to pink, more common in northern Rockies.

– not as above; flowers white; plant is

– robust, freely branched,
Porter Lovage
Ligusticum porteri

– slender, unbranched,
Hemlock Parsley
Conioselinum scopulorum

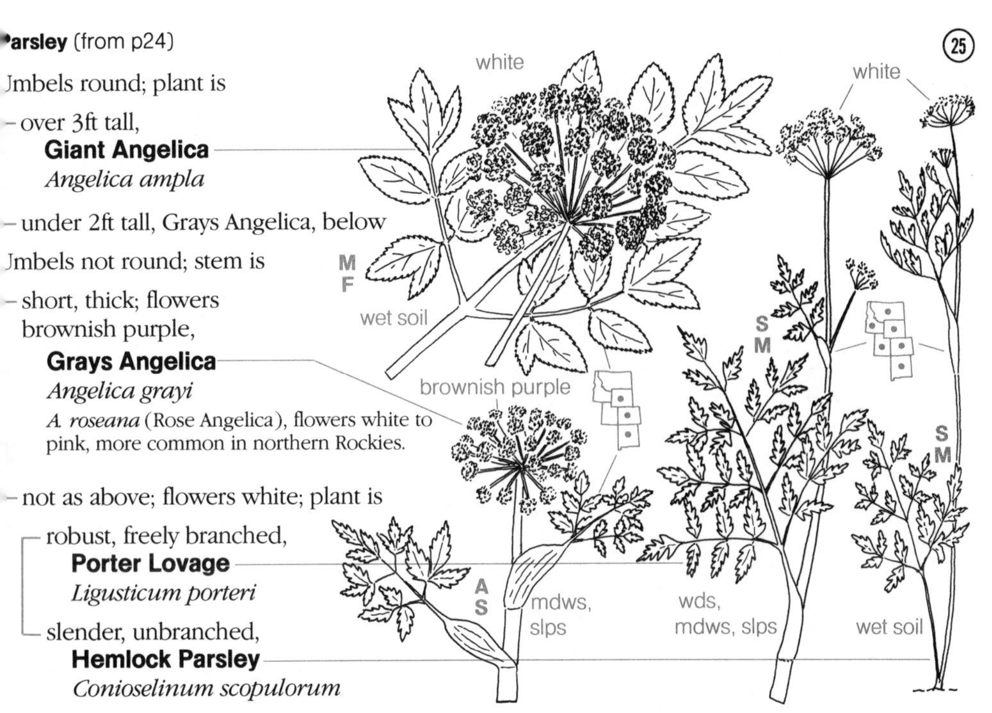
white
M
F
wet soil
brownish purple
A
S
mdws,
slps
white
S
M
wds,
mdws, slps
S
M
wet soil

DOGBANE FAMILY *(Apocynaceae)* Opposite entire leaves with milky juice. Flowers with five sepals, five united petals, five stamens. Two pistils with style and stigma united, ovaries separate.

Spreading Hemp

Apocynum androsaemifolium

A. cannabinum (Indian Hemp) flowers white, leaves erect

GINSENG FAMILY *(Araliaceae)* Plants with tiny regular flowers in umbels. Flower parts in fives, ovary inferior. Leaves compound, long petioled, growing from an underground rootstock.

Wild Sarsaparilla

Aralia nudicaulis

MILKWEED FAMILY *(Asclepiadaceae)* Herbs with opposite or whorled simple leaves, usually milky juice. Flowers regular, parts in fives, petal-like corona present between the petals and stamens. Two pistils with style and stigma united, ovaries separate. Flowers in umbels.

Showy Milkweed

Asclepias speciosa

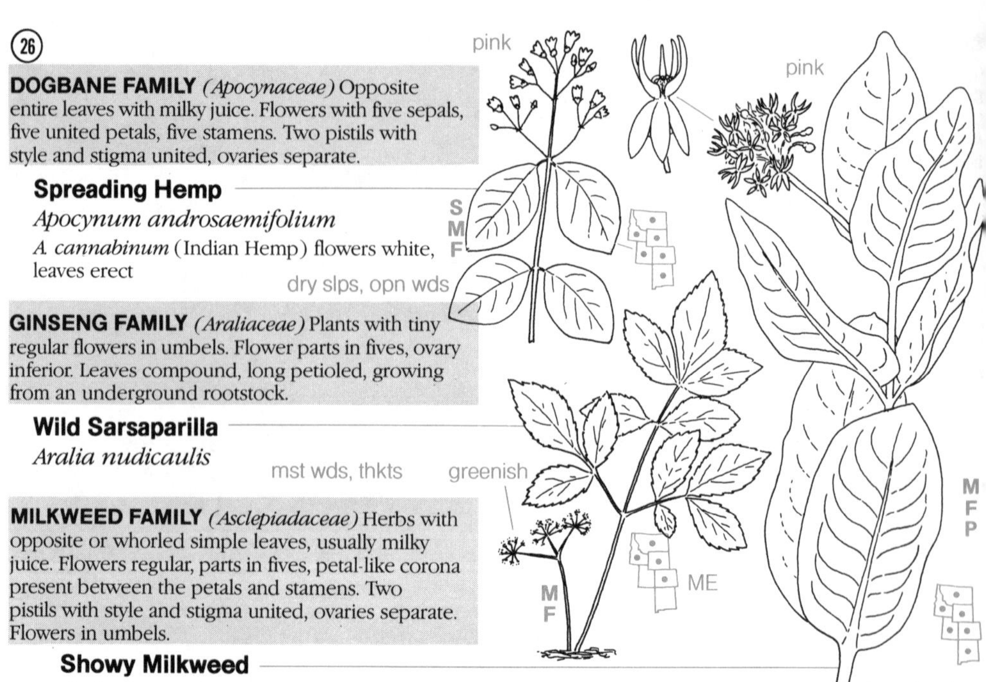
pink
S
M
F
dry slps, opn wds
pink
mst wds, thkts
greenish
M
F
ME
M
F
P
dist soil, rdsds

SUNFLOWER or ASTER FAMILY *(Asteraceae* or *Compositae)* Large family with small flowers tightly grouped into heads subtended by bracts. Flowers of two types, disk and ray. Petals united. Sepals modified into bristles or scales called pappus. Ovary inferior.

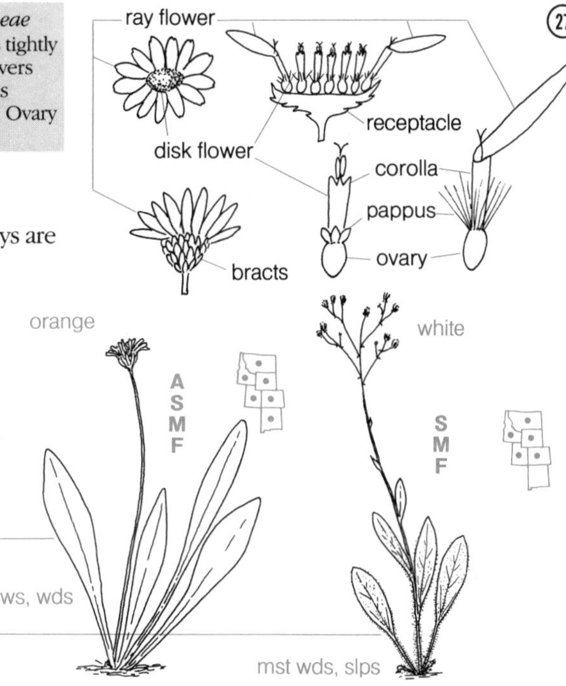
ray flower
disk flower
receptacle
corolla
pappus
ovary
bracts
orange
white
A
S
M
F
S
M
F
mdws, wds
mst wds, slps

Heads with both ray and disk flowers; rays are

– yellow or orange, p37

– not yellow, p45

Heads with disk flowers only, p31

Heads with ray flowers only; flowers

– pink, blue or blue-purple, next page.

– yellow, p29.

– orange,
Burnt-orange Dandelion
Agoseris aurantiaca

– white,
White Hawkweed
Hieracium albiflorum

(28) **Sunflower, ray only** (from p27)

Flowers pink,
Skeleton Weed
Lygodesmia sp.
L. grandiflora (Showy Skeleton Weed), illus.;
L. juncea, scale-like leaves, smaller heads.

Flowers sky blue on stick-like branches,
Chicory
Cichorium intybus

Flowers not as above,
Blue Lettuce
Lactuca tatarica var. *pulchella*

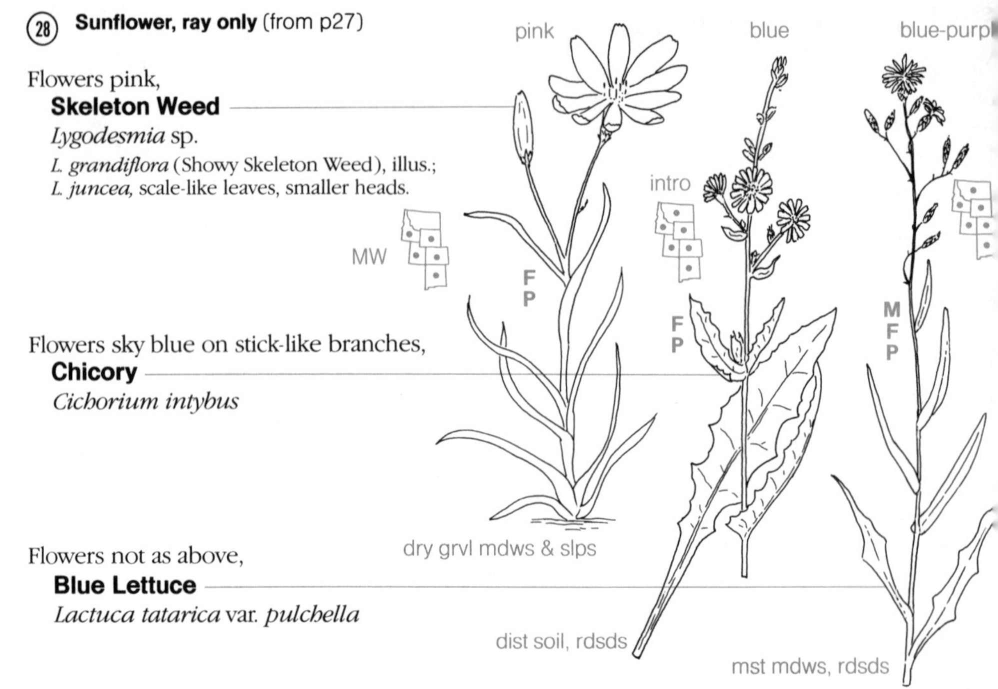
pink
blue
blue-purpl
MW
F
P
intro
F
P
M
F
P
dry grvl mdws & slps
dist soil, rdsds
mst mdws, rdsds

Sunflower, ray only (from p27)

More than one head per stem, next page.

One head per stem; stem leaves are

- present,
  Salsify
  Tragopogon dubius
- absent; lower bracts are
  - bent downward,
    Common Dandelion
    Taraxacum officinale
  - erect; leaf edges are
    - white hairy, often wavy,
      False Dandelion
      Nothocalais cuspidata
    - not as above,
      Tall False Dandelion
      Agoseris glauca

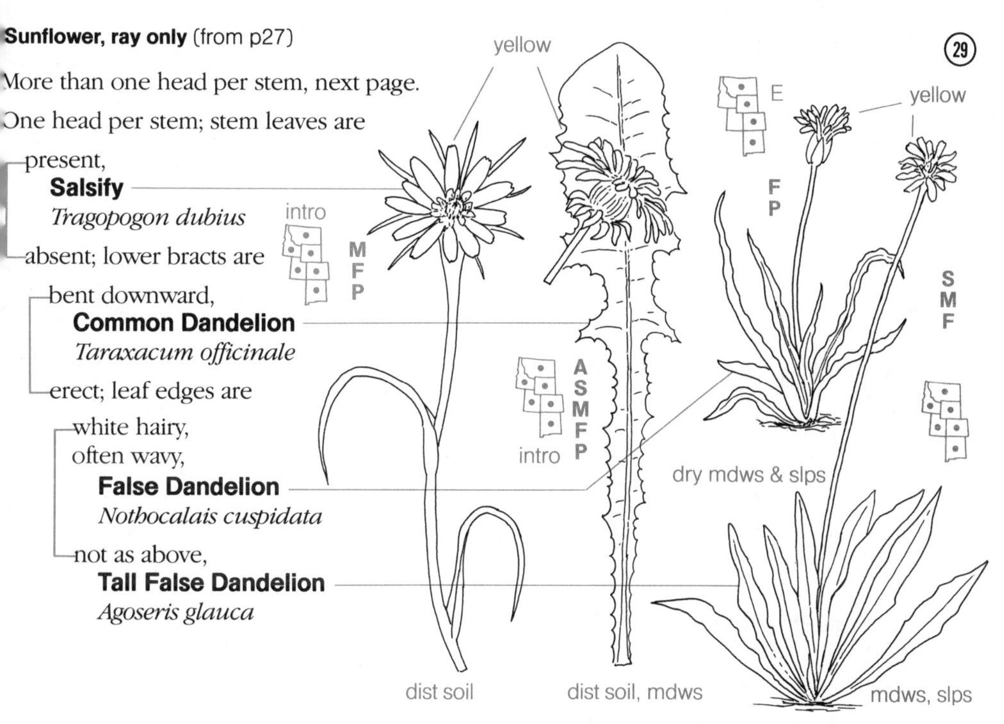
yellow
intro
M
F
P
dist soil
intro
A
S
M
F
P
dist soil, mdws
E
F
P
yellow
dry mdws & slps
S
M
F
mdws, slps

(30) Sunflower, ray only (from p29)

Leaves pinnately divided,
False Salsify
Scorzonera laciniata

Leaves simple; bracts have
- black hairs,
  Slender Hawkweed
  Hieracium gracilis
- not as above,
  Meadow Hawkbeard
  Crepis runcinata
  C. occidentalis, leaves gray hairy.

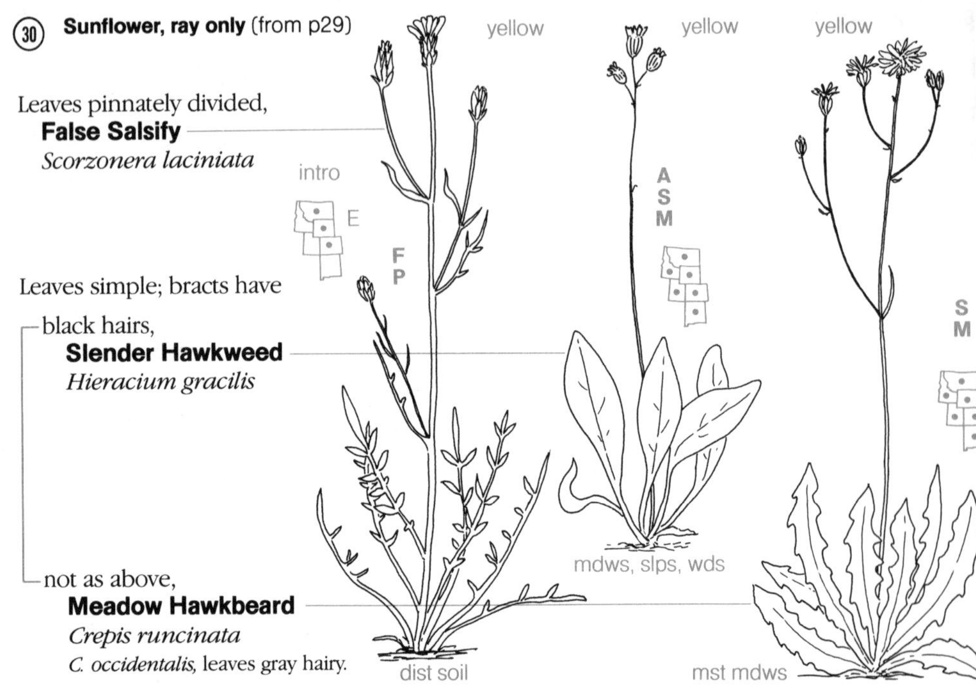
yellow
intro
E
F
P
dist soil
yellow
A
S
M
mdws, slps, wds
yellow
S
M
mst mdws

Sunflower, disk only (from p27)

Head not thistle-like; plant never spiny, next page

Head thistle-like; plant often spiny; leaves

- not spiny,

  Knapweed

  Centaurea sp.

  C. diffusa (Diffuse Knapweed), illus.; *C. maculosa* (Spotted Knapweed), flowers purple; *C. repens* (Russian Knapweed), bracts papery, flowers lavender.

- spiny, bracts are

  - broad, flat, spreading; pappus bristles not feathery,

    Musk Thistle

    Carduus nutans

  - not as above; pappus bristles feathery,

    Thistle

    Cirsium sp.

    C. arvense (Canada Thistle), illus., is introduced, has small purple heads. Native thistles include *C. centaureae, C. coloradense, C. undulatum,* others.

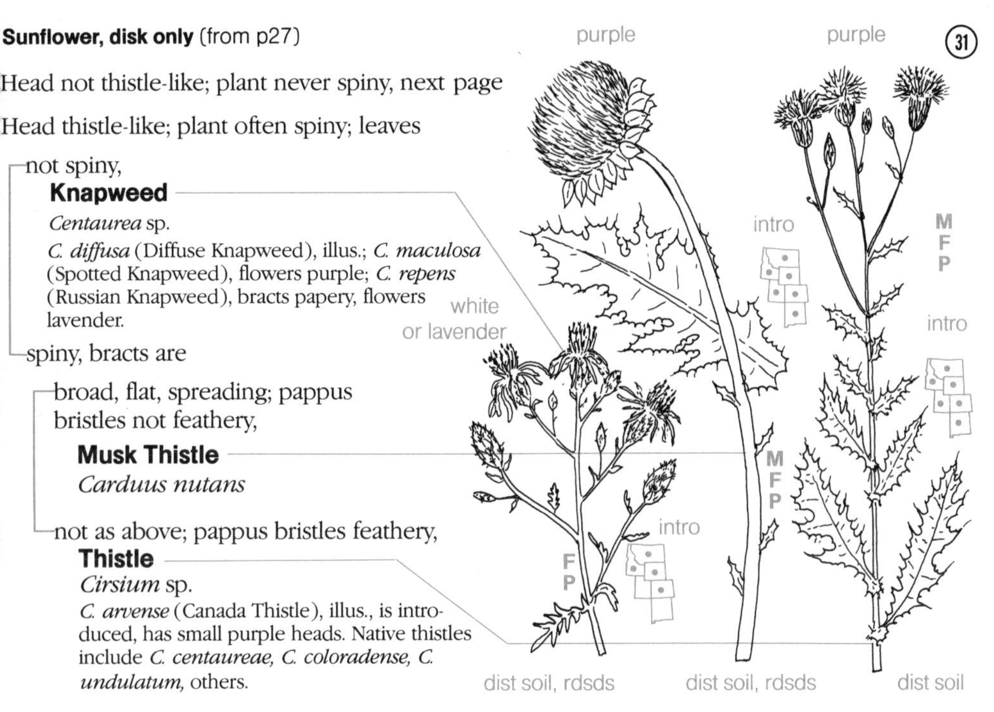

white
or lavender
intro
F
P
dist soil, rdsds
purple
intro
M
F
P
dist soil, rdsds
purple
M
F
P
intro
dist soil

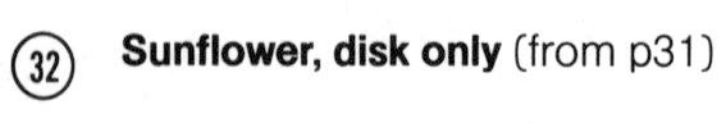

(32) **Sunflower, disk only** (from p31)

Head not cone shaped, next page.

Head cone shaped; leaves are

- finely divided; crushed head smells like pineapple,
  Pineapple Weed
  Chamomilla suaveolens

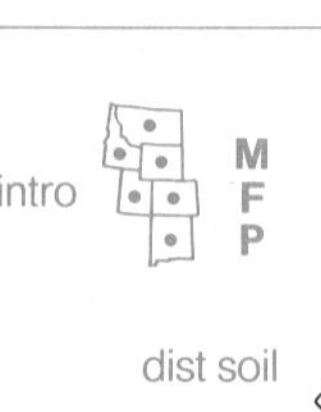
intro
M
F
P

greenish yellow
dist soil

- not as above,
  Rayless Cone Flower
  Rudbeckia occidentalis
  R. occidentalis var. *montana,* leaves divided.

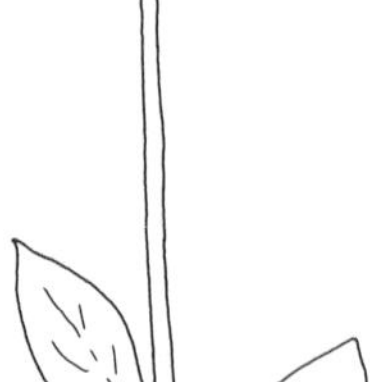
dark purp
mst mdws, wds, aspn

MW
M

Sunflower, disk only (from p32)

Heads white, pale yellow, cream or pink, p35

Heads purple to lavender,
Blazing Star
Liatris punctata

Heads bright yellow; leaves are
- simple, next page.
- divided or cleft; bracts are
  - united,
    Rayless Greenthread
    Thelesperma megapotamicum
  - separate; heads
    - one per stem,
      Gold Buttons
      Erigeron compositus var. *discoideus*
    - not as above,
      Woolly Hymenopappus
      Hymenopappus filifolius

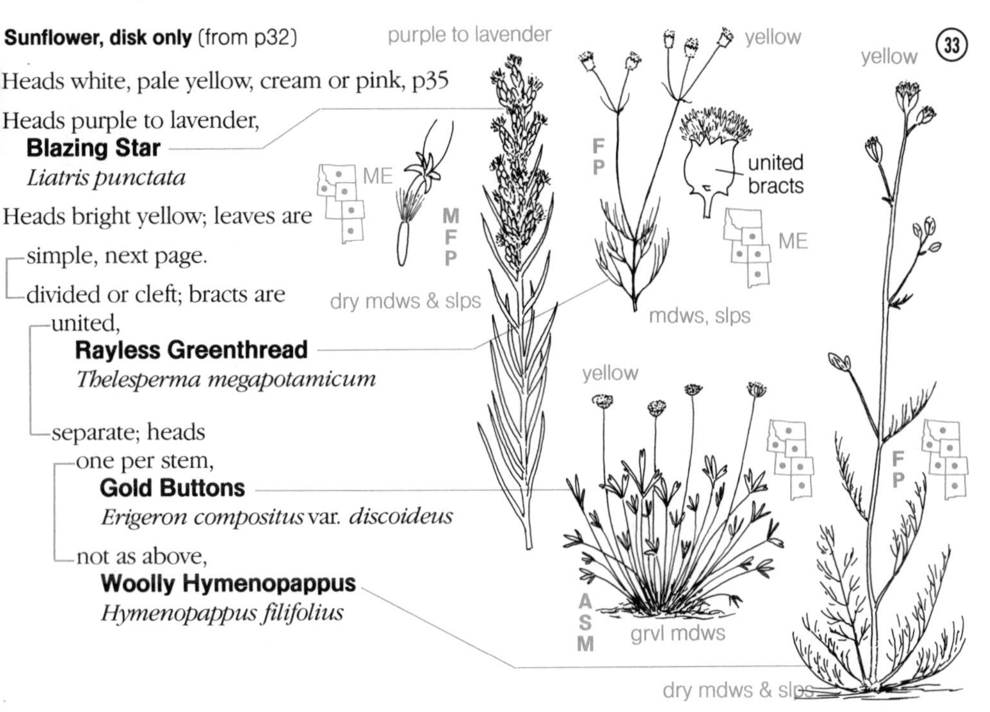
purple to lavender
ME
M F P
dry mdws & slps
yellow
F P
united bracts
ME
mdws, slps
yellow
F P
yellow
A S M
grvl mdws
dry mdws & slps

34 Sunflower, disk only (from p33)

Leaves opposite,
Rayless Arnica
Arnica parryi

Leaves alternate; heads

fleshy,
Bigelow Groundsel
Senecio bigelovii

not fleshy,
Nodding Senecio
Senecio pudicus

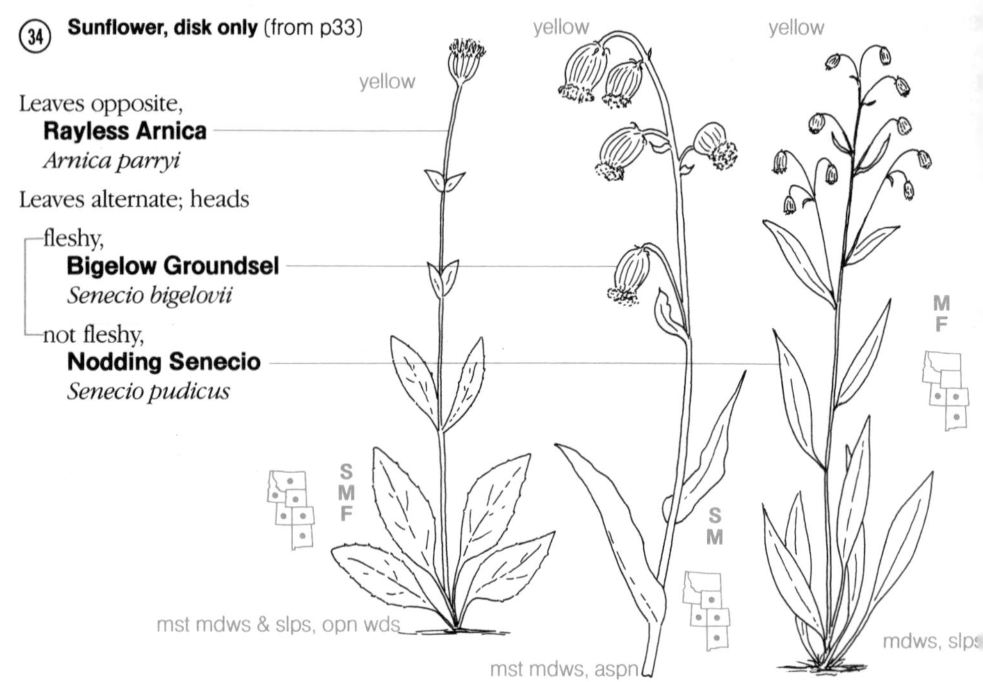
yellow
yellow
yellow
S
M
F
mst mdws & slps, opn wds
S
M
mst mdws, aspn
M
F
mdws, slps

Sunflower, disk only (from p33)

Bracts not papery, next page.

Bracts papery, plant is

– mat forming; bracts white or pink,

Pussytoes

Antennaria sp.

A. parvifolia (Sun-loving Pussytoes), bracts seldom pink; *A. microphylla* (Rosey Pussytoes), illus., bracts often pink.

– not mat forming; bracts white; leaves are

– greatly reduced up stem and have three prominent veins,

Tall Pussytoes

Antennaria pulcherrima

– not greatly reduced up stem and have one to three prominent veins,

Pearly Everlasting

Anaphalis margaritacea

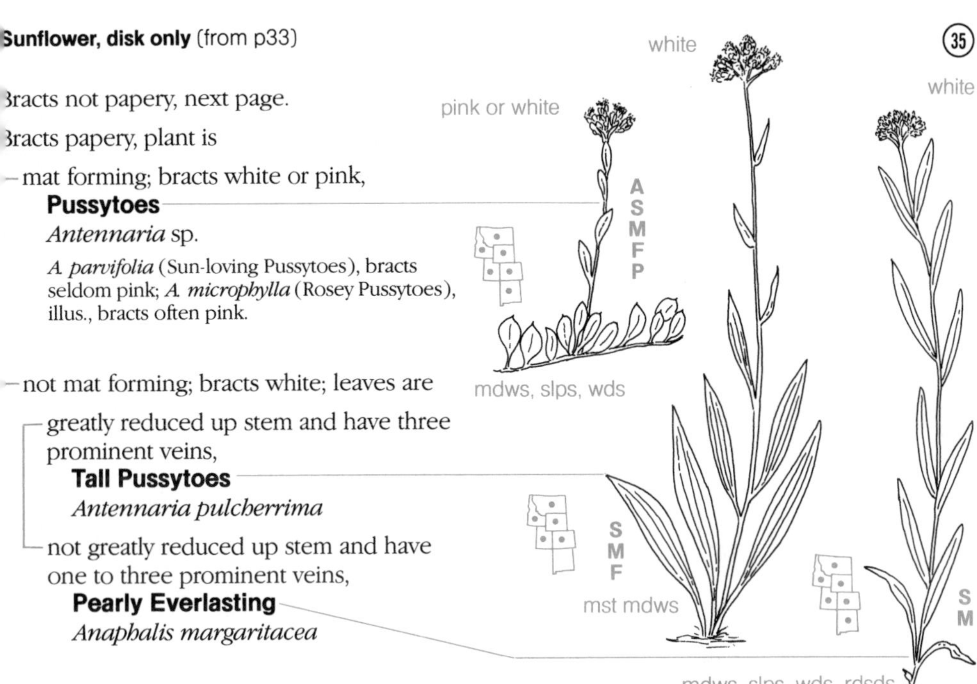
white
white
pink or white
A
S
M
F
P
mdws, slps, wds
S
M
F
mst mdws
S
M
mdws, slps, wds, rdsds

(36) **Sunflower, disk only** (from p35)

Leaves triangular,
Tasselflower
Brickellia grandiflora

Leaves not triangular; flower heads are

—tiny; pappus absent,
Sage
Artemisia sp.
A. frigida (Fringed Sage), illus., finely divided, silvery leaves; *A. ludoviciana* (Prairie Sage), white-hairy, entire or lobed leaves; many others.

—larger; pappus composed of scales; leaf segments are

—long, narrow, thread-like,
Cream Tips
Hymenopappus tenuifolius

—not as above,
Dusty Maiden
Chaenactis douglasii

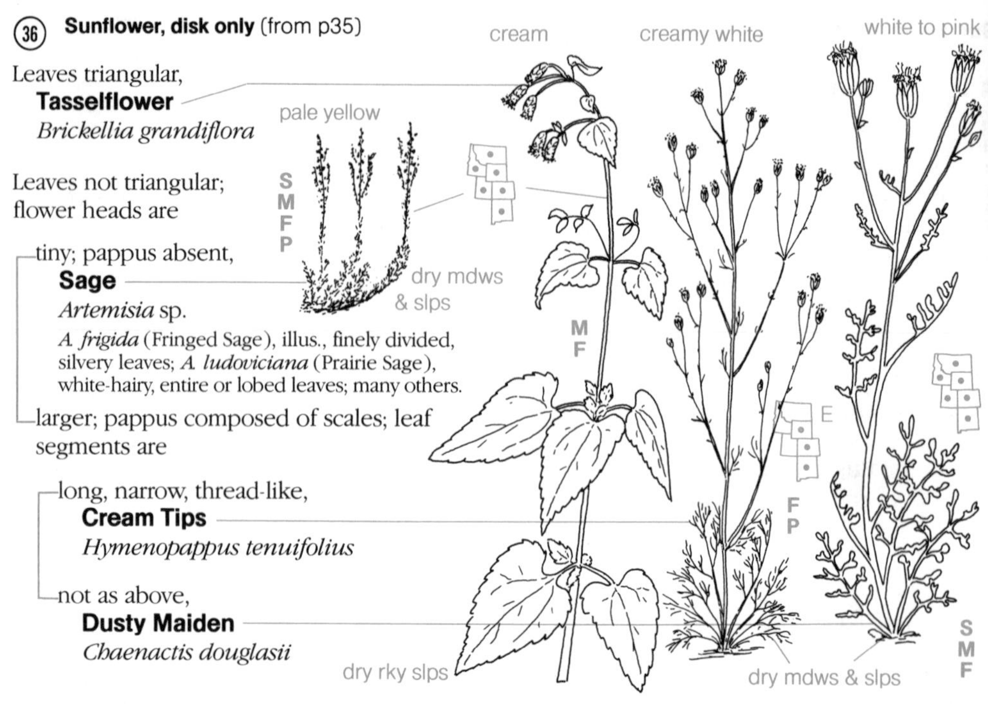

cream
creamy white
white to pink
pale yellow
S
M
F
P
dry mdws & slps
M
F
E
F
P
dry rky slps
dry mdws & slps
S
M
F

Sunflower, ray and disk, yellow (from p 27)

Leaves alternate or basal, p39.

Leaves opposite (at least on lower stem), and are

—divided into long, narrow segments,
Greenthread
Thelesperma filifolium

—undivided; pappus is

—composed of long, fine bristles (easy to see),
Arnica
Arnica sp.
A. cordifolia (Heart-leaved Arnica), illus., has heart-shaped leaves; *A. chamissonis; A. fulgens; A. latifolia; A. longifolia;* others.

—absent; receptacle cone-shaped,
Sun Spots
Viguiera multiflora

—composed of two scales next page.

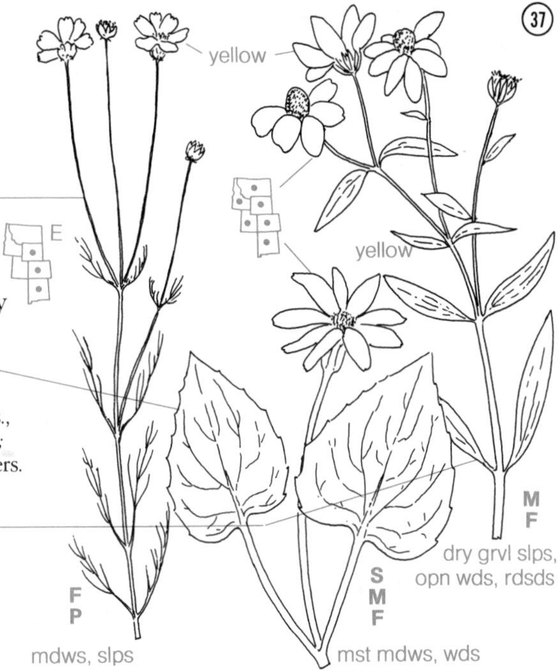

yellow
E
F
P
mdws, slps
yellow
S
M
F
mst mdws, wds
M
F
dry grvl slps, opn wds, rdsds

(38) **Sunflower, ray and disk, yellow** (from p37)

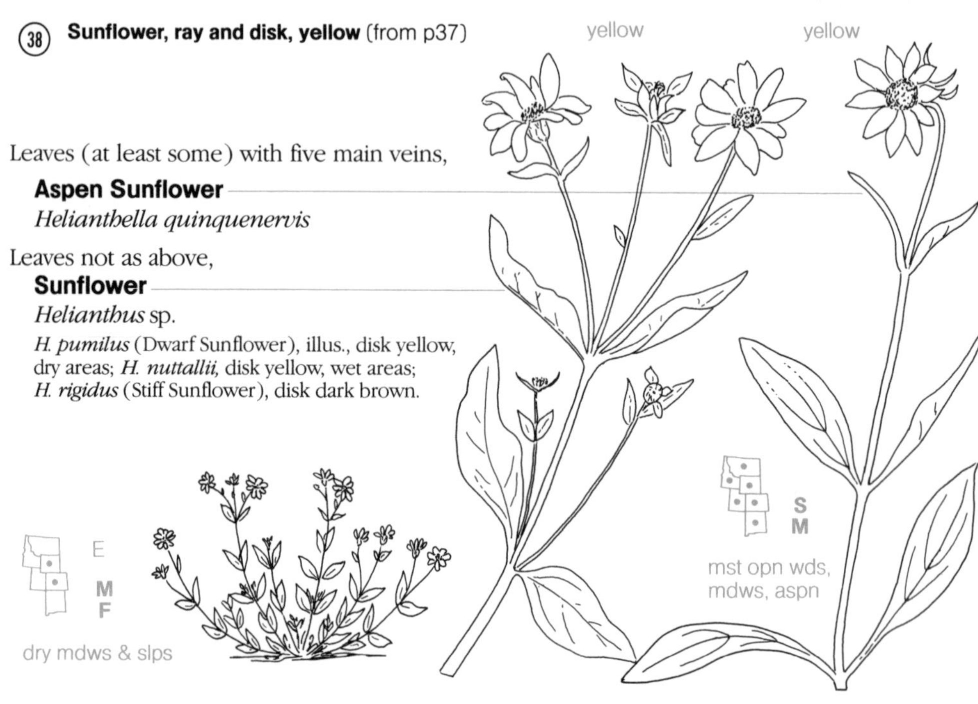
yellow
yellow
E
M
F
dry mdws & slps
S
M
mst opn wds,
mdws, aspn

Leaves (at least some) with five main veins,

Aspen Sunflower
Helianthella quinquenervis

Leaves not as above,

Sunflower
Helianthus sp.

H. pumilus (Dwarf Sunflower), illus., disk yellow, dry areas; *H. nuttallii,* disk yellow, wet areas; *H. rigidus* (Stiff Sunflower), disk dark brown.

Sunflower, ray and disk, yellow (from p37)

Head very elongate,
Cone Flower
Ratibida columnifera

Head not as above; disk flowers are

– yellow, light brown to greenish, next page.

– red or reddish,
Blanket Flower
Gaillardia aristata
G. pinnatifida (Pinnate-leaf Gaillardia), leaves pinnately divided, s CO, NM, UT.

– dark brown, black or purplish; disk is

mound shaped,
Black-eyed Susan
Rudbeckia hirta

flat or slightly mound shaped,
Sunflower
Helianthus sp.
H. annuus (Common Sunflower), illus., bracts fringed; *H. petiolaris* (Prairie Sunflower), lacks fringe. Hybrids occur.

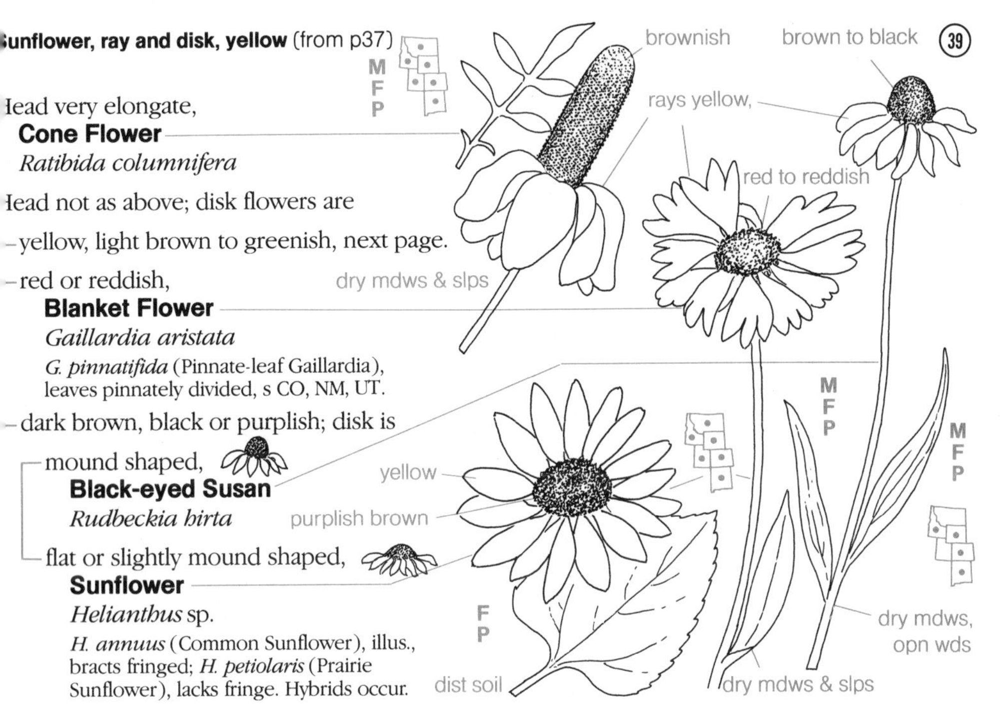
M
F
P
brownish
brown to black
rays yellow,
red to reddish
dry mdws & slps
M
F
P
M
F
P
yellow
purplish brown
F
P
dist soil
dry mdws & slps
dry mdws,
opn wds

Sunflower, ray and disk, yellow (from p39)

Stem leaves present, next page.

Stem leaves absent (a few very reduced leaves may be present); leaves are

- compound,
  Hoary Balsamroot
  Balsamorhiza incana
- simple, shaped like
  - arrowhead,
    Arrowleaf Balsamroot
    Balsamorhiza sagittata
  - not as above,
    Perky Sue
    Hymenoxys acaulis

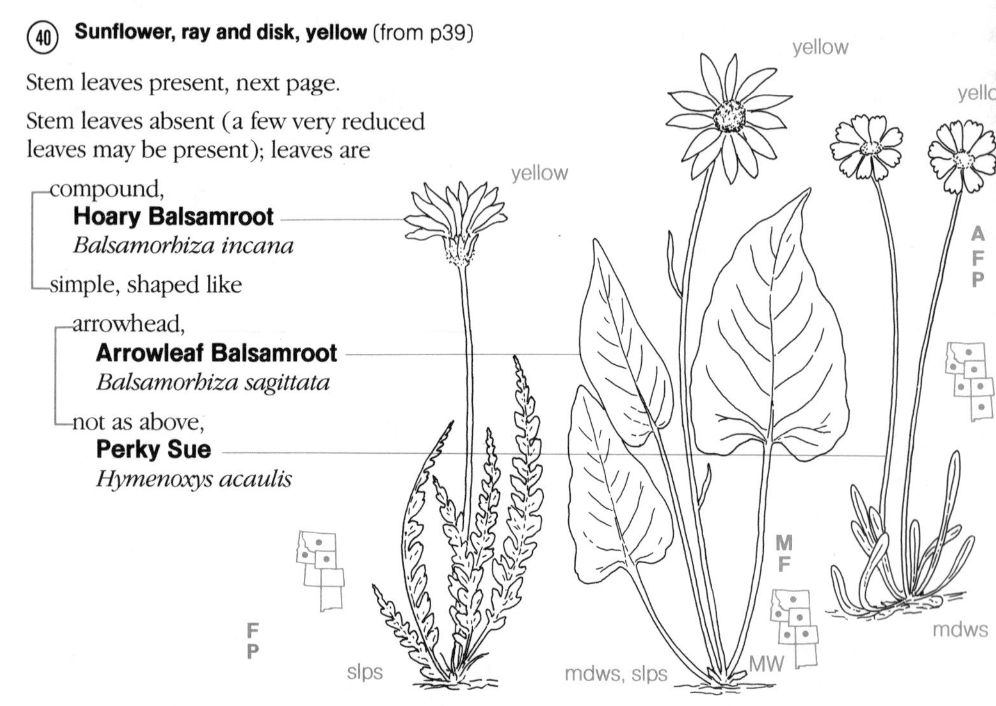
yellow
F
P
slps
yellow
M
F
mdws, slps
MW
yello
A
F
P
mdws

Sunflower, ray and disk, yellow (from p40)

Leaves simple, next page.

Leaves compound or divided; leaf segments are

—large; heads cone-shaped,
Goldenglow
Rudbeckia laciniata var. *ampla*

—narrow, thread-like; bracts are

—hairy; base of basal leaves woolly-hairy,
Colorado Rubber Plant
Hymenoxys richardsonii

—not hairy,
Broom Senecio
Senecio spartioides

—not as above,
Ragleaf Bahia
Bahia dissecta

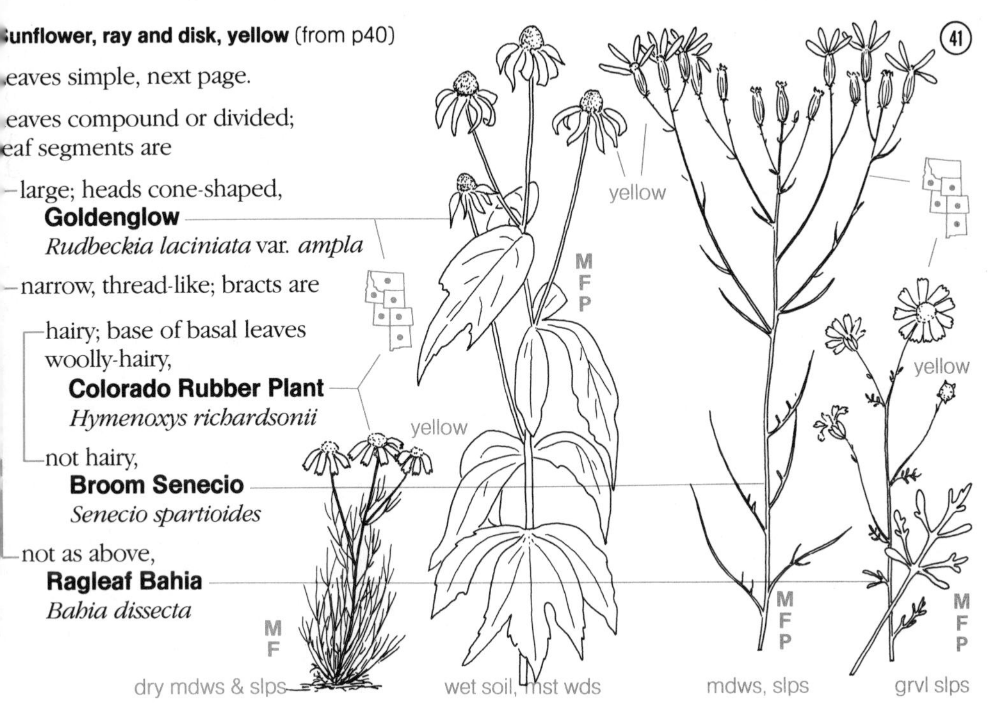
yellow
yellow
yellow
M F P
M F
M F P
M F P
dry mdws & slps
wet soil, mst wds
mdws, slps
grvl slps

(42) **Sunflower, ray and disk, yellow** (from p41)

Bracts sticky, curled,

Gumweed

Grindelia sp.

G. squarrosa, plains and lower foothills, *G. subalpina* (Mountain Gumweed) illus., foothills to subalpine.

Bracts all about equal length, narrow except for a few tiny bracts present at base of head,

Senecio

Senecio sp.

S. triangularis (Triangle-leaved Senecio), illus.; *S. atratus; S. eremophilus; S. fendleri; S. integerrimus; S. spartioides* (illus. p41); others.

Bracts not as above, next page.

yellow
yellow
M
F
E
dry mdws & slps
S
M
F
wet soil

Heads ⅛ - ¼ in long, numerous,

Goldenrod

Solidago sp.

S. canadensis; S. multiradiata, illus.; *S. nana; S. sparsiflora;* others.

Heads not as above; plant

–with many stems which commonly have spreading hairs; heads an inch wide or less; pappus in two series, inner of long bristles, outer of tiny bristles or scales,

Golden Aster

Heterotheca sp.

H. villosa, illus., low elevations; *H. fulcrata,* montane, subalpine, WY, CO.

–not as above; rays are

–about ¼ in. long or less,

Parry Goldenweed

Haplopappus parryi

–longer, next page.

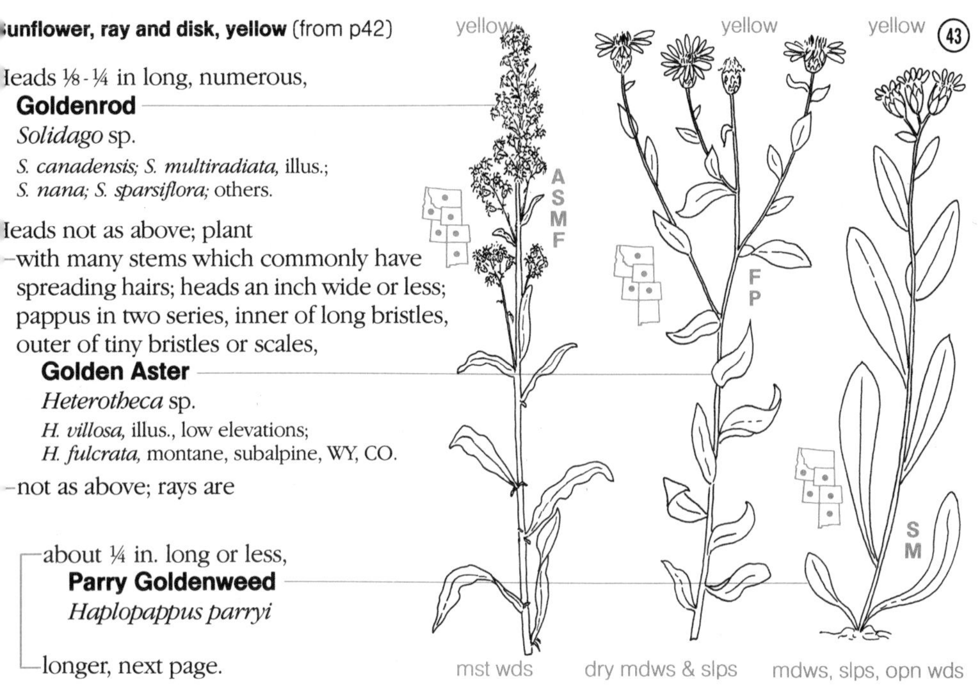
yellow
A
S
M
F
mst wds
yellow
F
P
dry mdws & slps
yellow
S
M
mdws, slps, opn wds

Sunflower, ray and disk, yellow (from p43)

Heads several, clustered at top of single stem,

Orange Sneezeweed

Dugaldia hoopesii

Heads solitary or few per stem; rays are

- narrow, less than ⅛ in. wide, curled on older heads,

  Golden Curleyhead

  Haplopappus croceus

- wider, not curled,

  Mules Ear

  Wyethia amplexicaulis

  W. arizonica (Arizona Mules Ear), upper leaves petioled.

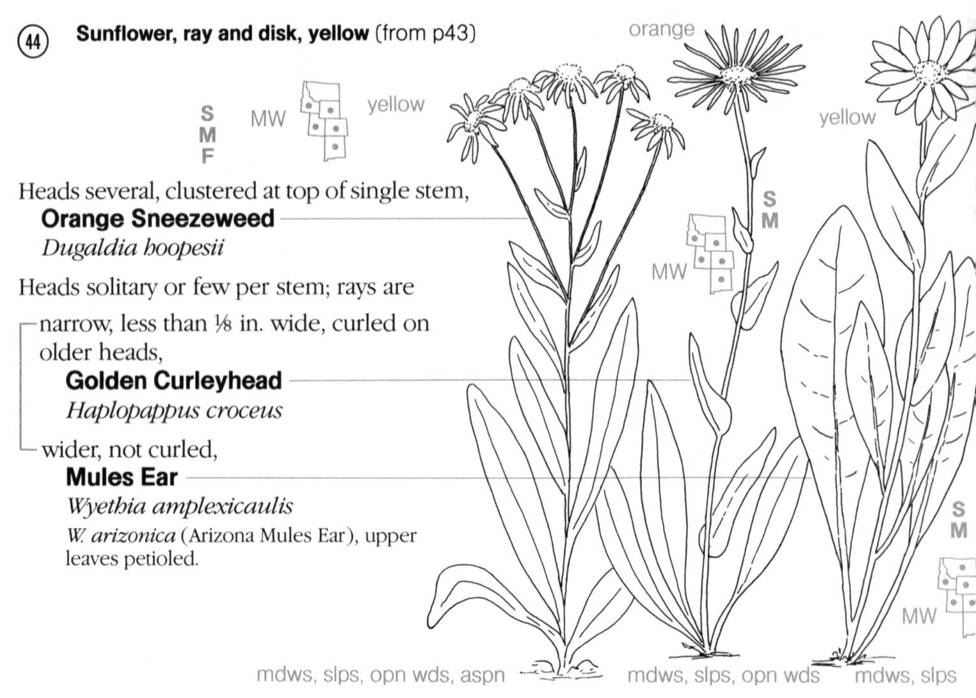
S
M
F
MW
yellow
mdws, slps, opn wds, aspn
orange
S
M
MW
mdws, slps, opn wds
yellow
S
M
MW
mdws, slps

Sunflower, ray and disk, not yellow (from p27)

Leaves not finely divided into many segments, next page.

Leaves finely divided into many segments, fern-like; disk flowers are

—yellow,
Chamomile
Matricaria perforata

—white; heads are

—tiny, in flat-topped clusters,
Yarrow
Achillea millefolium var. *lanulosa*

—not as above,
Wild Cosmos
Leucampyx newberryi

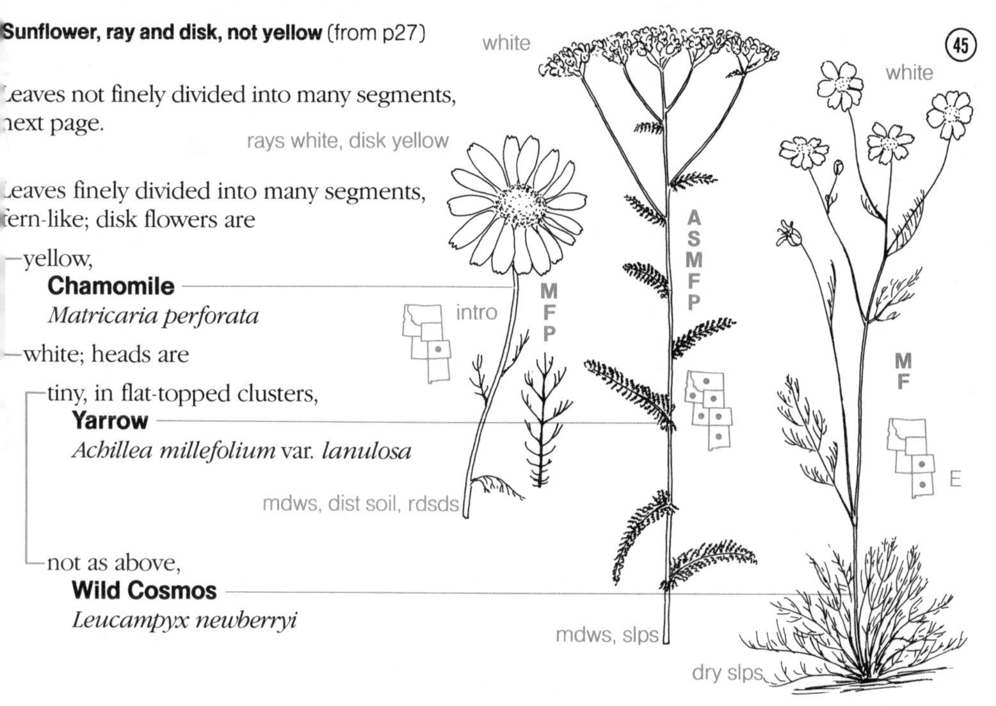
rays white, disk yellow
intro
M
F
P
mdws, dist soil, rdsds
white
A
S
M
F
P
mdws, slps
white
M
F
E
dry slps

(46) **Sunflower, ray and disk, not yellow** (from p45)

Heads 3in or more wide,
White Mules Ear
Wyethia helianthoides

Heads smaller; plant is

—stemless or with combination of short stems and large heads; pappus of stiff bristles,
Easter Daisy
Townsendia sp.
Stemless: *T. exscapa* illus., and *T. hookeri.* Short-stemmed: *T. grandiflora* , *T. eximia*, s CO, NM, and *T. parryi,* ID, WY.

—not as above; head is

—very elongate,
Cone Flower
Ratibida columnifera

—not as above, next page.

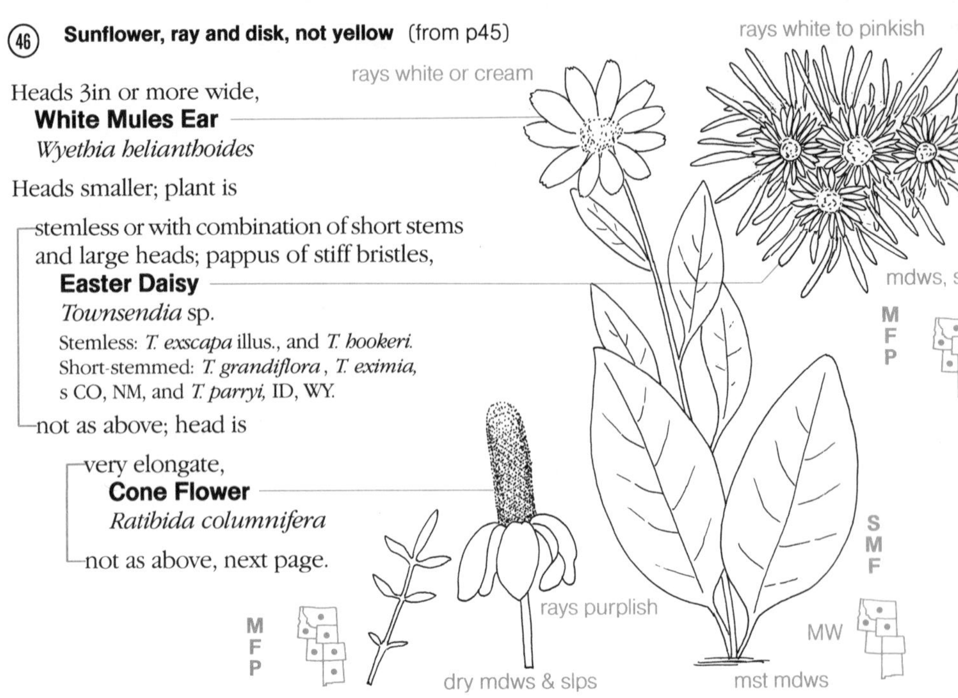
rays white to pinkish
rays white or cream
mdws, sl
M
F
P
S
M
F
rays purplish
MW
M
F
P
dry mdws & slps
mst mdws

rays purple

Bracts curled, sticky,

Tansy Aster

Machaeranthera bigelovii

A S M F P

Bracts about equal length,

Daisy

Erigeron sp.

E. compositus; E. divergens; E. flagellaris; E. melanocephalus; E. peregrinus; E. speciosus; many others.

S M F P

rays white, pink, blue or purple

dry or mst mdws, slps, wds

grvl slps, mdws

Bracts overlap like shingles; heads are

— over 1in wide; rays white; bracts brown-edged; pappus absent,

Ox-eye Daisy

Leucanthemum vulgare

M F

— not as above; pappus of soft bristles,

Aster

Aster sp.

A. chilensis; A. ericoides; A. hesperius; A. laevis; A. porteri; many others.

A S M F P

dist soil, rdsds

BORAGE FAMILY *(Boraginaceae)* Herbs with flowers often in coiled clusters. Flowers regular with five united petals. Ovary superior, four-lobed, maturing into four nutlets. Leaves simple, usually alternate. Plants often bristly or hairy.

Flowers white or blue next page.

Flowers red-purple,
Houndstongue
Cynoglossum officinale

Flowers yellow or orange; inflorescence has

stiff, spreading hairs,
Golden Cryptantha
Cryptantha flava

not as above,
Narrow-leaf Puccoon
Lithospermum incisum
L. multiflorum (Many-flowered Puccoon), petal edges entire; *L. ruderale* (Stoneseed), flowers hidden by leaves.

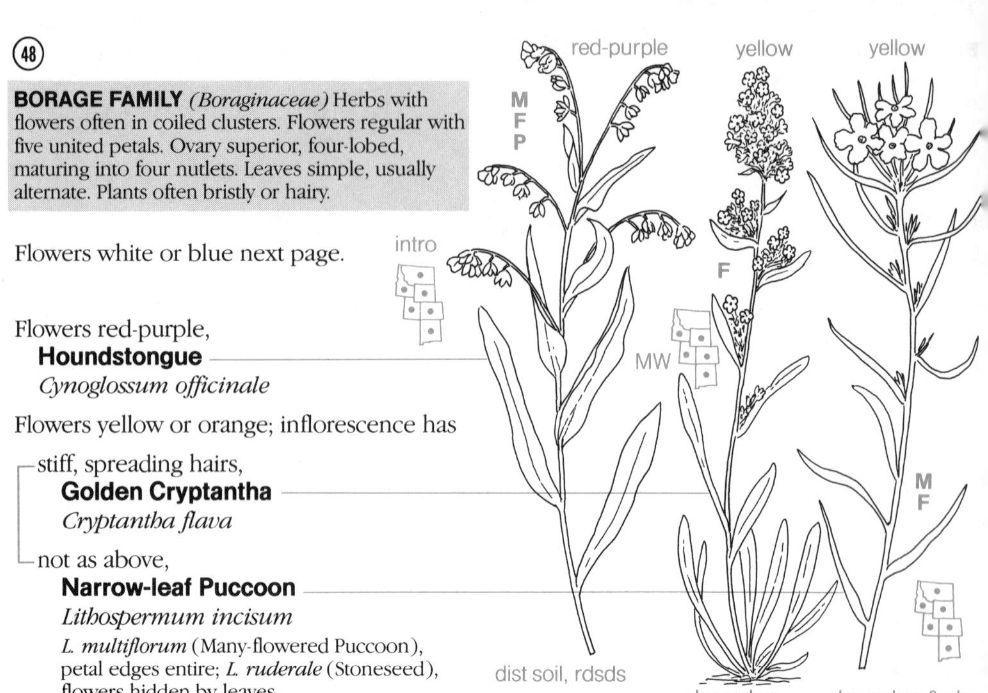
red-purple
M
F
P
intro
dist soil, rdsds
yellow
F
MW
dry mdws
yellow
M
F
dry mdws & slps

Petal lobes point inward,

Marble Seed

Onosmodium molle var. *occidentale*

Petal lobes not as above; plant is

- spike-like,

  Miners Candle

  Cryptantha virgata

- not spike-like; flowers are

  - nodding in loose clusters,

    Chiming Bells

    Mertensia sp.

    M. ciliata (Tall Chiming Bells), illus., tall plant, wet areas; *M. lanceolata* (Lanceleaf Chiming Bells), smaller plant, dry areas.

  - not as above, next page.

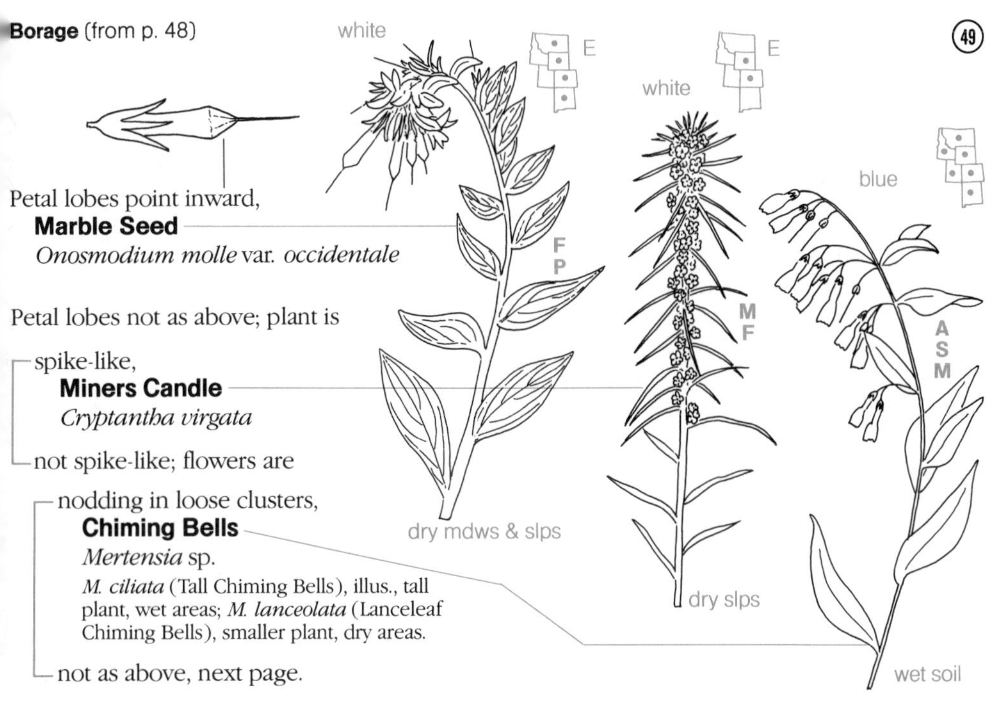
white
E
F
P
dry mdws & slps
white
E
M
F
dry slps
blue
A
S
M
wet soil

(50) **Borage** (from p49)

Nutlets prickly; bract is

- present beneath each flower; pedicel erect in fruit,
  Beggars Tick
  Lappula redowskii
- absent; pedicel bent downward in fruit,
  False Forget-me-not
  Hackelia floribunda

Nutlets smooth; flowers are

- blue,
  Mountain Forget-me-not
  Myosotis alpestris
- white,
  Cryptantha
  Cryptantha sp.
  C. fendleri, illus.; *C. jamesii; C. minima;* others.

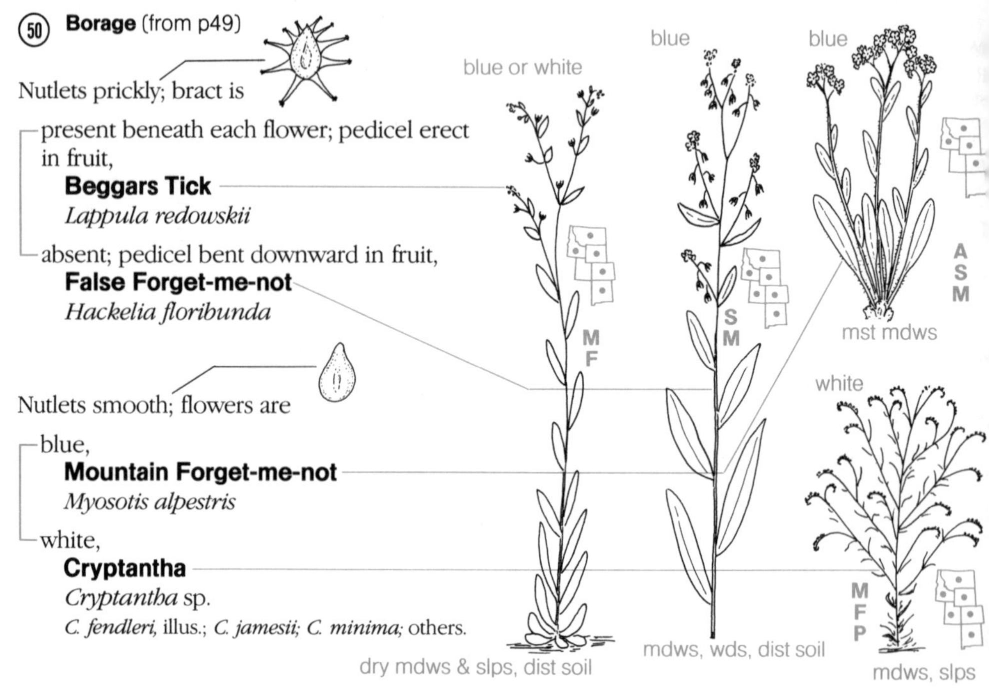
blue or white
M
F
dry mdws & slps, dist soil
blue
S
M
mdws, wds, dist soil
blue
A
S
M
mst mdws
white
M
F
P
mdws, slps

MUSTARD FAMILY *(Brassicaceae or Cruciferae)*
Regular flowers with four sepals, four petals, six stamens, superior ovary. The fruits (seed pods) necessary for identification are found below the flowers.

Flowers not yellow, p55.

Flowers yellow; fruit is

—short, not more than three times as long as wide, p53.

—longer; flowers are

—in long showy raceme,
Princes Plume
Stanleya pinnata

—not as above, flowers are

—less than ½ in. wide, next page.

—larger,
Western Wallflower
Erysimum asperum

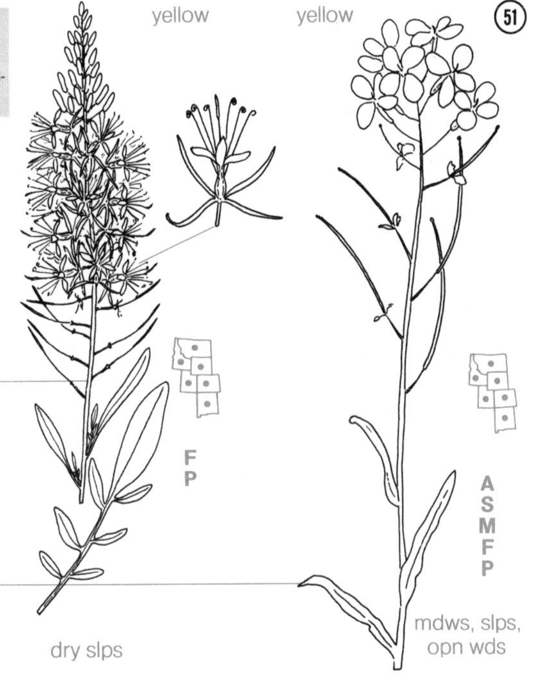
yellow
yellow
F
P
A
S
M
F
P
dry slps
mdws, slps,
opn wds

Mustard (from p51)

All leaves simple, entire or with small teeth,
Draba
Draba sp. (illus. p53)

Leaves (at least lower ones) compound or deeply lobed, with segments of upper leaves

- narrow, nearly thread-like,
  Jim Hill Mustard
  Sisymbrium altissimum
- not as above; leaves
  - have large terminal lobe, and are
    - glaucous (white-coated),
      Field Mustard
      Brassica campestris
    - not glaucous,
      Wintercress
      Barbarea orthoceras
  - not as above,
    Tansy Mustard
    Descurainia sp.
    D. richardsonii, D. pinnata, D. sophia, illus.

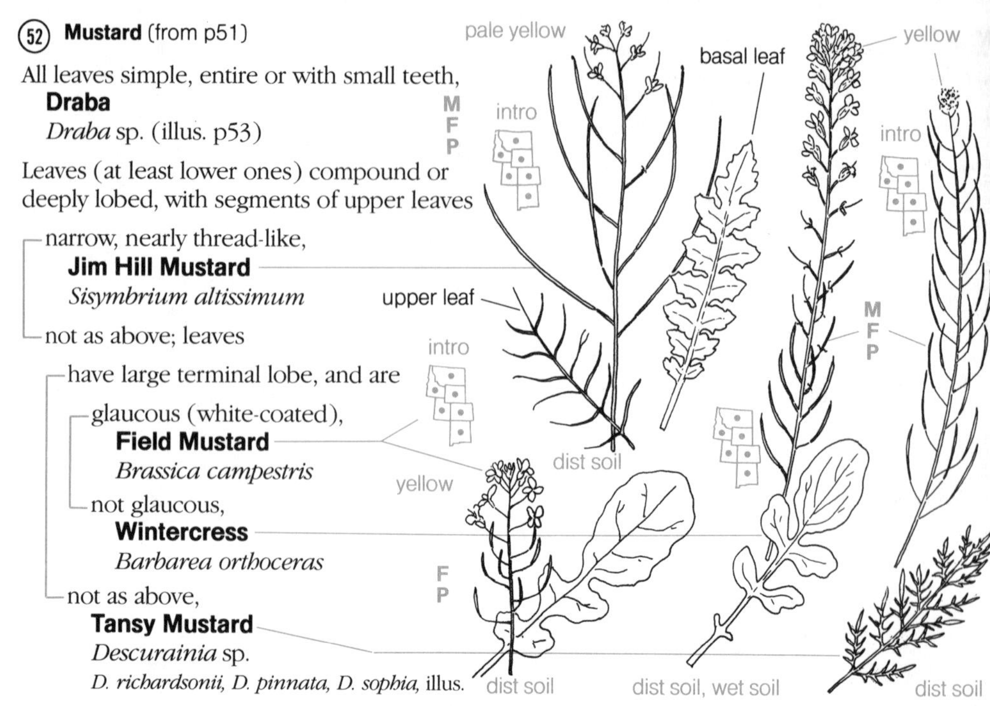
M
F
P
pale yellow
intro
upper leaf
basal leaf
yellow
intro
M
F
P
intro
dist soil
yellow
F
P
dist soil
dist soil, wet soil
dist soil

Mustard (from p51)

Fruit not flattened or only slightly so, often inflated, next page.

Fruit flattened, and

—round in face view,

Wild Alyssum

Alyssum sp.

A. minus, illus.; *A. alyssoides,* sepals remain on mature fruit.

—not as above,

Draba

Draba sp.

D. aurea, illus.; *D. crassifolia; D. streptocarpa* (Twisted-pod Draba); others.

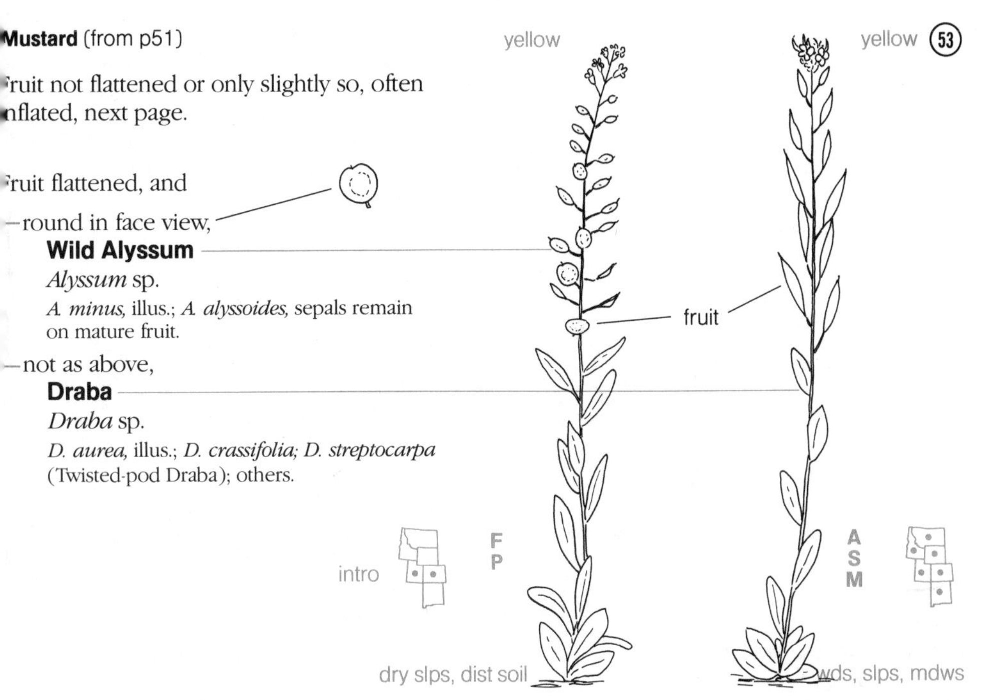
yellow
yellow
fruit
intro
F
P
A
S
M
dry slps, dist soil
wds, slps, mdws

54 **Mustard** (from p53)

Plant of moist areas,

Cress

Rorippa sp.

R. teres illus.; *R. curvipes* var. *alpina; R. palustris* ssp. *bispida; R. sinuata;* others.

Plant of dry areas; fruit is

—double; some basal leaves fiddle-shaped,

Double Bladderpod

Physaria vitulifera

—single,

Mountain Bladderpod

Lesquerella montana

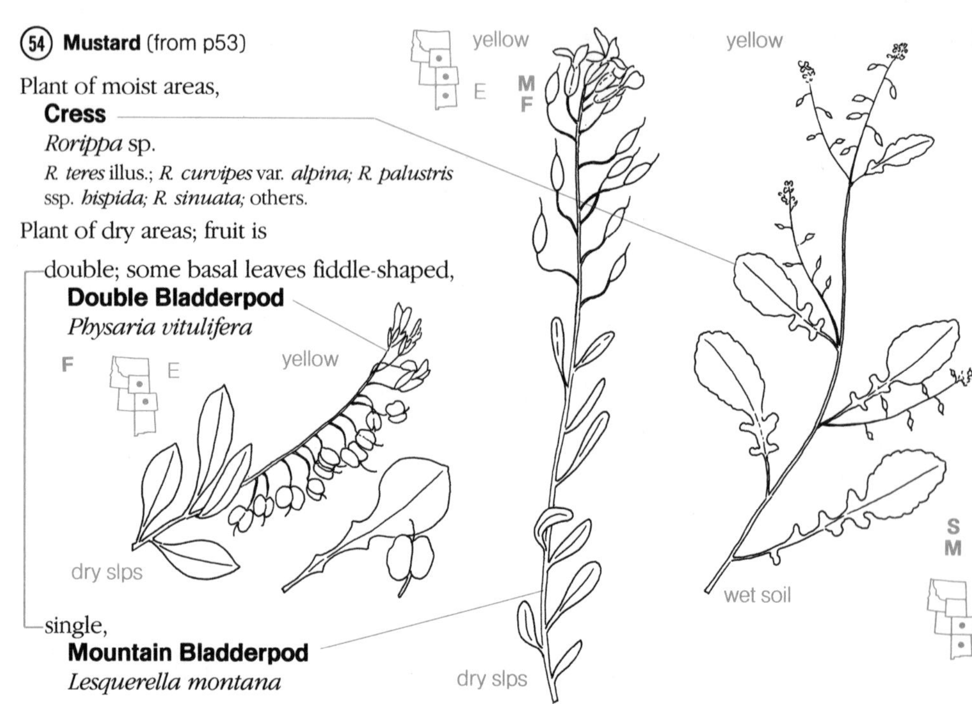

yellow
E
M
F
yellow
F
E
yellow
dry slps
dry slps
wet soil
S
M

Mustard (from p51)

Fruits short, less than three times as long as wide, p57.

Fruits longer; base of leaf is

—clasping stem,
Rockcress
Arabis sp.
A. divaricarpa, A. fendleri, illus., *A. hirsuta,* others.

—not as above; flowers are

—pink, lavender or purple, next page.

—white; leaves are

—simple,
Brookcress
Cardamine cordifolia

—compound,
Watercress
Nasturtium officinale

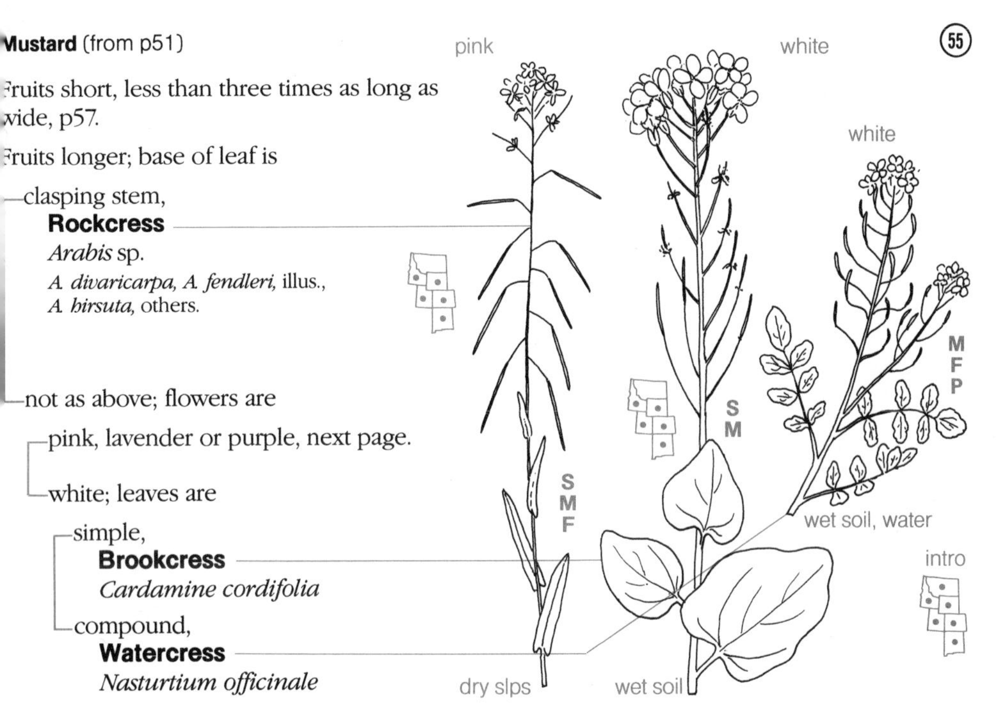
pink
S
M
F
dry slps
white
S
M
wet soil
white
M
F
P
wet soil, water
intro

56 **Mustard** (from p55)

Fruit flattened; flowers large, showy,
Dames-Violet
Hesperis matronalis

Fruit and flowers not as above,
Blue Mustard
Chorispora tenella

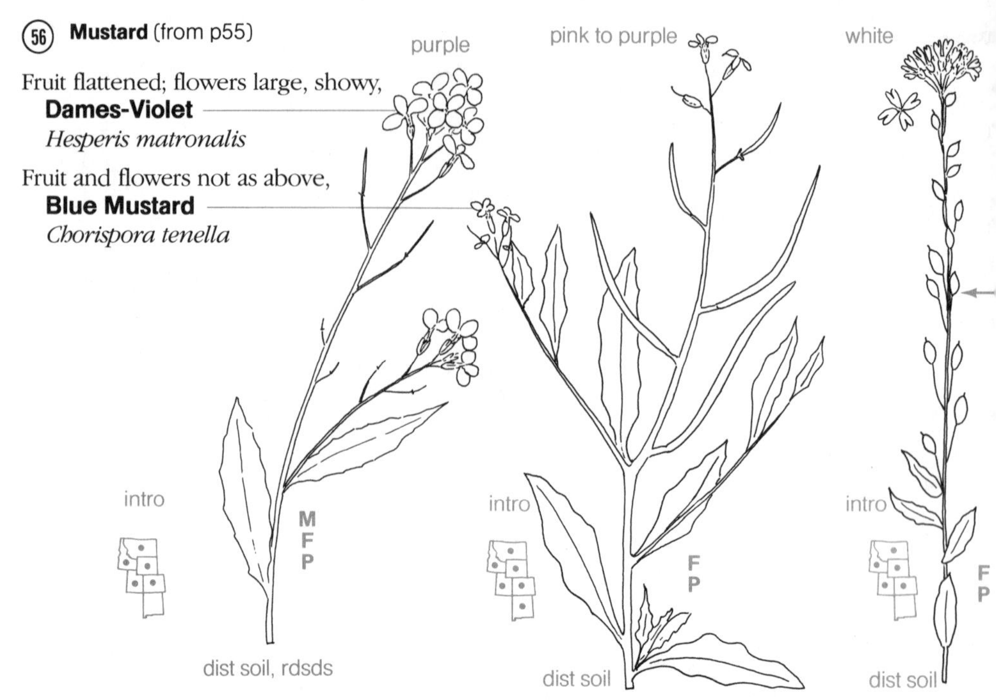
purple
pink to purple
white
intro
MFP
dist soil, rdsds
intro
FP
dist soil
intro
FP
dist soil

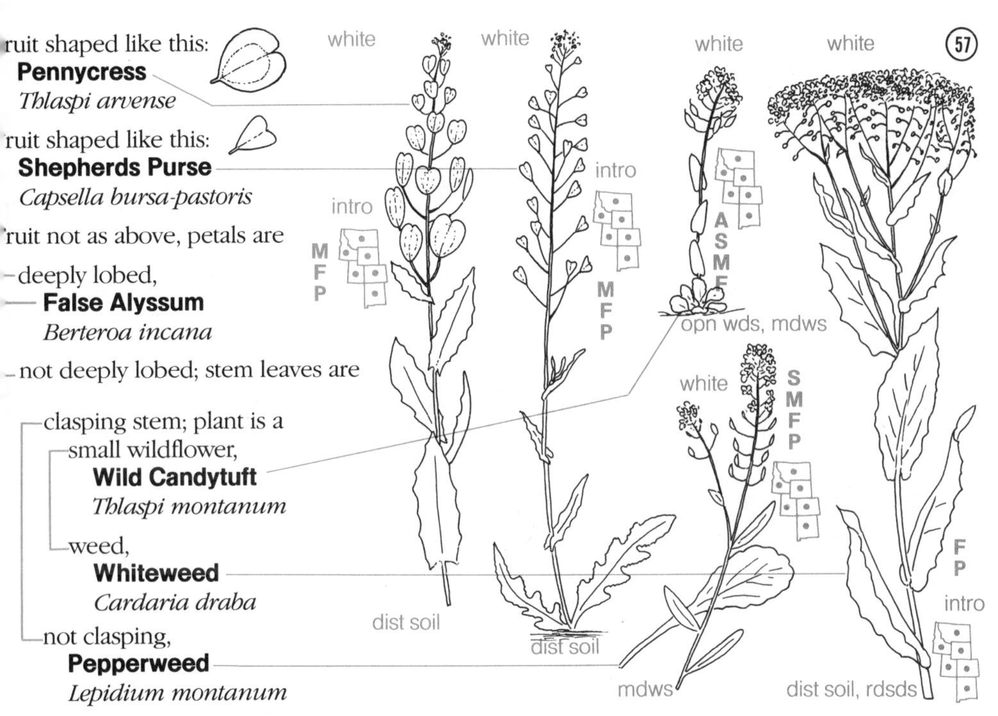
ruit shaped like this:
Pennycress
Thlaspi arvense
ruit shaped like this:
Shepherds Purse
Capsella bursa-pastoris
ruit not as above, petals are
deeply lobed,
False Alyssum
Berteroa incana
not deeply lobed; stem leaves are
clasping stem; plant is a
small wildflower,
Wild Candytuft
Thlaspi montanum
weed,
Whiteweed
Cardaria draba
not clasping,
Pepperweed
Lepidium montanum
white
intro
M
F
P
dist soil
white
intro
M
F
P
dist soil
white
A
S
M
F
opn wds, mdws
white
S
M
F
P
mdws
white
57
F
P
intro
dist soil, rdsds

CACTUS FAMILY *(Cactaceae)* Succulent spiny leafless plants with showy regular flowers. Sepals, petals, stamens many. Ovary inferior.

Plant in one piece, not jointed; flowers are

- pink or greenish yellow, next page.
- red,
  Kingscrown Cactus
  Echinocereus triglochidiatus var. *melanacanthus*

Plant composed of joints which are

- flat,
  Plains Pricklypear
  Opuntia polyacantha
- round in cross section,
  Brittle Cactus
  Opuntia fragilis

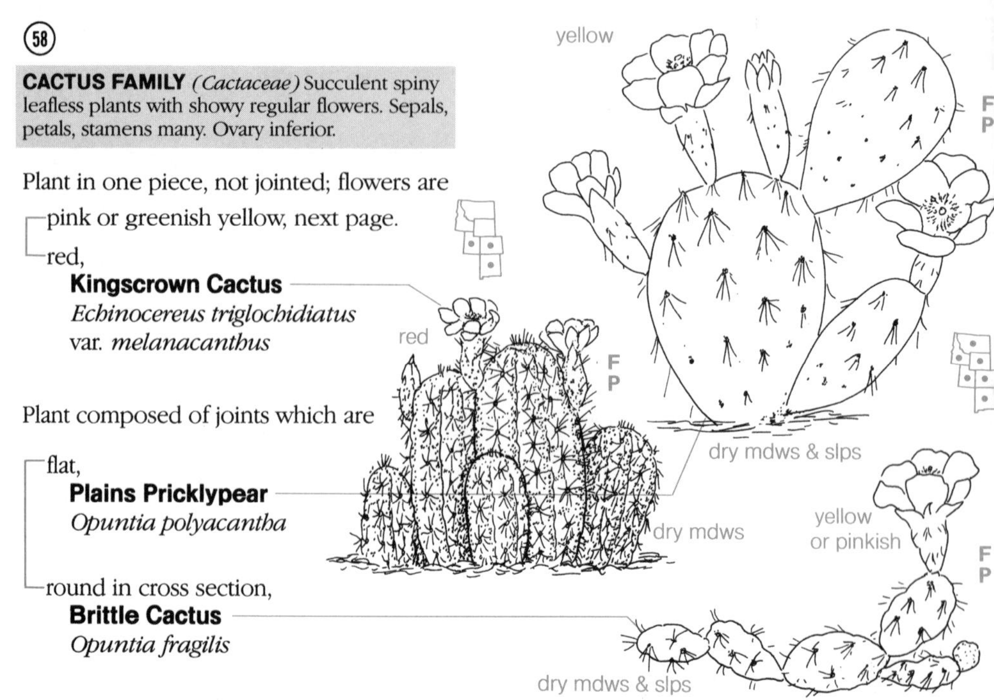
yellow
F
P
red
F
P
dry mdws & slps
dry mdws
yellow
or pinkish
F
P
dry mdws & slps

Cactus (from p58)

Flowers pink, and

— fragrant,
Mountain Ball Cactus
Pediocactus simpsonii

— not fragrant,
Ball Nipple Cactus
Coryphantha vivipara

Flowers greenish yellow; sides of cactus have

— nipple-like projections,
Mesa Nipple Cactus
Coryphantha missouriensis

— vertical ridges,
Hen-and-Chickens
Echinocereus viridiflorus

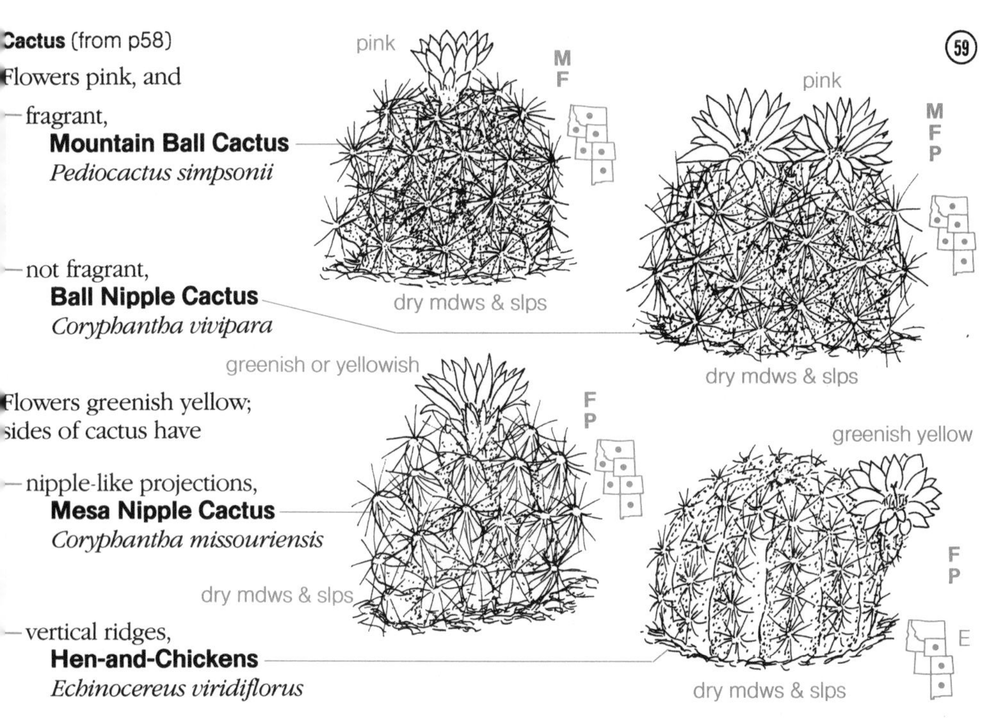
pink
M
F
dry mdws & slps
pink
M
F
P
dry mdws & slps
greenish or yellowish
F
P
dry mdws & slps
greenish yellow
F
P
E
dry mdws & slps

BELLFLOWER FAMILY *(Campanulaceae)*
Flowers regular or irregular with five united petals, five stamens, inferior ovary. Flowers often blue or purplish, bell-like. Leaves alternate, simple.

Upper leaves oval,
Venus Looking-glass
Triodanis perfoliata

Upper leaves not oval; flowers are

—nodding,
Mountain Harebell
Campanula rotundifolia

—erect, solitary,
Parry Harebell
Campanula parryi

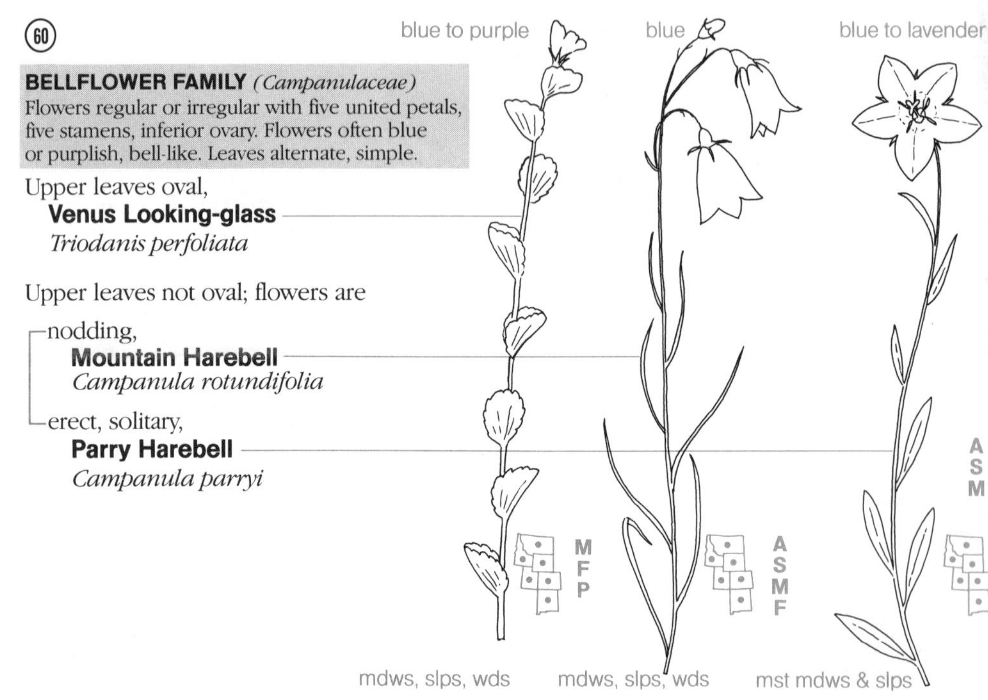
blue to purple
blue
blue to lavender
M F P
A S M F
A S M
mdws, slps, wds
mdws, slps, wds
mst mdws & slps

CAPER FAMILY *(Capparidaceae)* Flowers regular with four petals, four sepals, six to many stamens extending beyond the petals. Ovary superior. Leaves palmately compound.

Rocky Mountain Bee Plant

Cleome serrulata

C. lutea (Yellow Bee Plant), flowers yellow.

pink

M
F
P

dist soil, rdsds

HONEYSUCKLE FAMILY *(Caprifoliaceae)* Mostly shrubs and vines with opposite leaves. Flowers regular or irregular with five united petals, five stamens. Ovary inferior.

Twinflower

Linnaea borealis

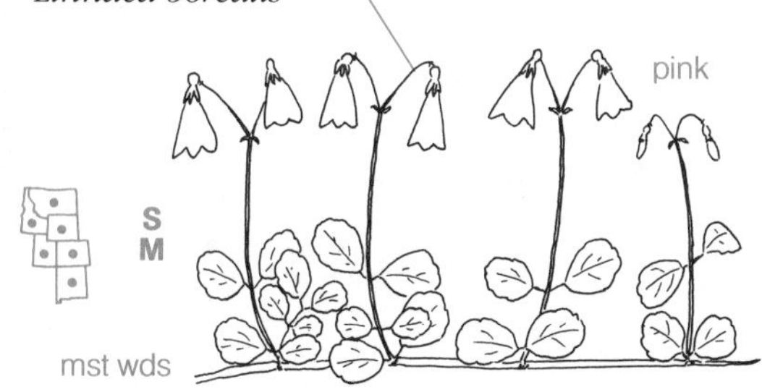

pink

S
M

mst wds

PINK FAMILY *(Caryophyllaceae)* Herbs with opposite entire leaves, often swollen nodes. Flowers regular, petals five, separate, stamens ten. Ovary superior.

Sepals separate next page.

Sepals united; plant is

- sticky on stems and/or calyx inflated,
  Cockle, Catchfly
  Silene sp.
  S. alba, illus., unisexual; *S. drummondii;*
  S. scouleri ssp. *hallii,* flowers pinkish;
  S. laciniata (Indian Pink), flowers red, NM;
  S. antirrhina; S. menziesii; S. noctiflora; others.

- not sticky; calyx not inflated,
  Bouncing Bet
  Saponaria officinalis

white

intro

M
F
P

dist soil

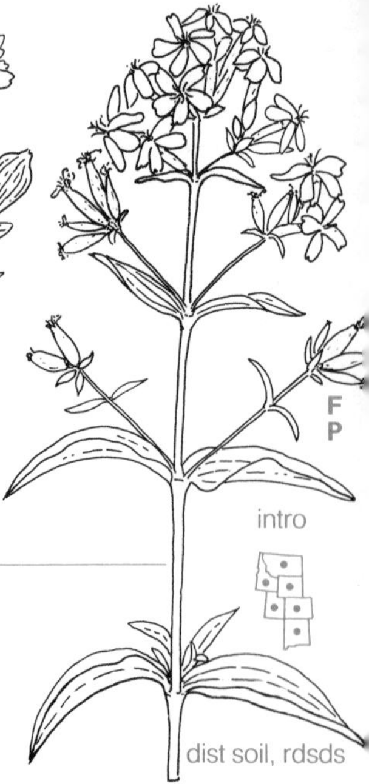

pale pink

F
P

intro

dist soil, rdsds

etals not deeply two-lobed, next page.

etals deeply two-lobed; leaves are

–over 2in long,

James Starwort

Stellaria jamesiana

–shorter, flowers are

–showy,

Mouse-ear Chickweed

Cerastium arvense

–inconspicuous,

Starwort

Stellaria sp.

S. longipes, illus.; *S. longifolia.*

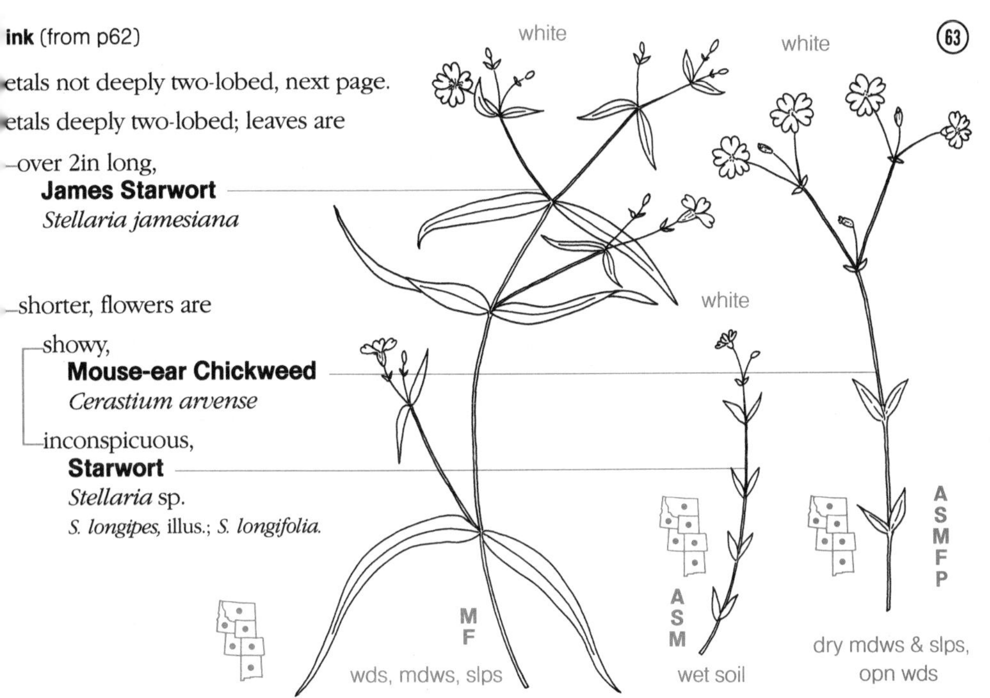
white
white
white
M
F
wds, mdws, slps
A
S
M
wet soil
A
S
M
F
P
dry mdws & slps,
opn wds

(64) **Pink** (from p63)

Flowers pink,
Sand Spurry
Spergularia rubra

Flowers white and
—in dense cluster,
Ballhead Sandwort
Arenaria congesta
—not as above,
Fendler Sandwort
Arenaria fendleri

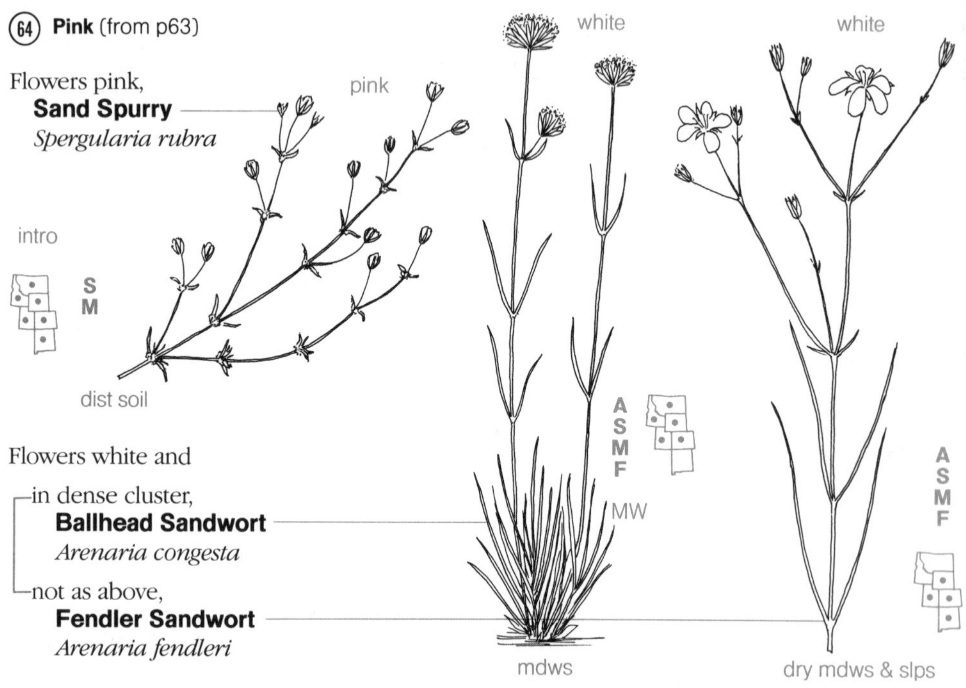
pink
intro
S
M
dist soil
white
A
S
M
F
MW
mdws
white
A
S
M
F
dry mdws & slps

GOOSEFOOT FAMILY *(Chenopodiaceae)*

lowers mostly unisexual, inconspicuous. Fruit may ecome showy. Many species are considered weeds.

Strawberry Blite or Squawpaint
Chenopodium capitatum

SPIDERWORT FAMILY *(Commelinaceae)*

Regular r irregular flowers with three petals, three sepals. eaves thick, rather succulent with sheathing bases. vary superior.

Western Spiderwort
Tradescantia occidentalis

MORNING GLORY FAMILY *(Convolvulaceae)*

ostly vines with simple leaves. Flowers regular, unnel-shaped with five united petals, five stamens, uperior ovary.

Field Bindweed
Convolvulus arvensis

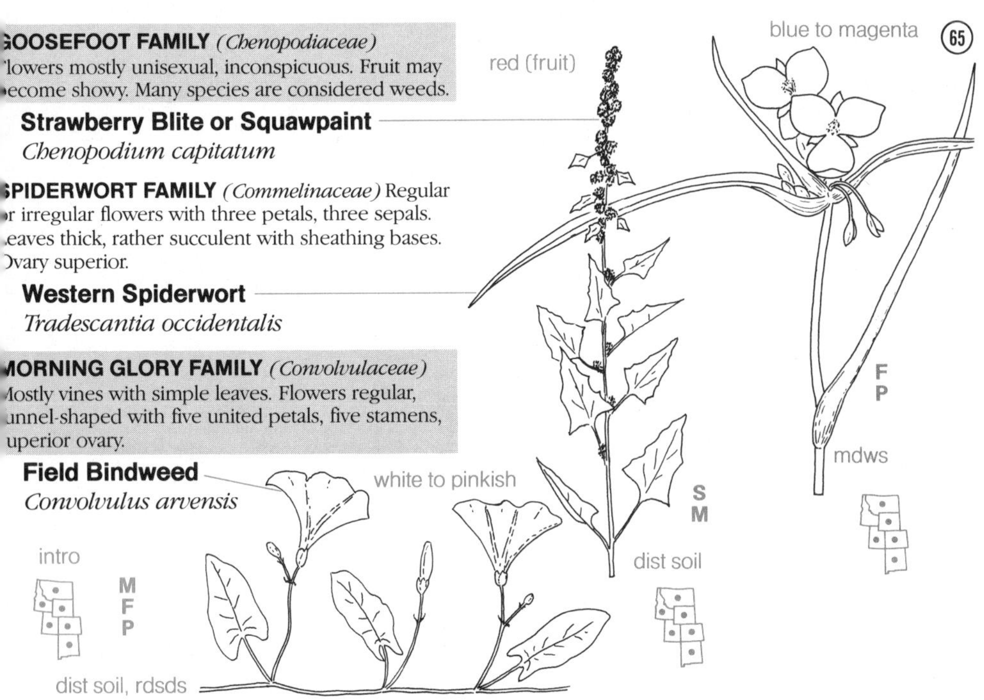
red (fruit)
blue to magenta
F
P
mdws
S
M
dist soil
white to pinkish
intro
M
F
P
dist soil, rdsds

STONECROP FAMILY *(Crassulaceae)* Succulent herbs with star-like flowers with four or five pointed separate petals, four or five pistils slightly united at base.

Flowers yellow,
Yellow Stonecrop
Sedum lanceolatum

yellow

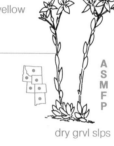

A S M F P

dry grvl slps

Flowers pink, in rounded cluster,
Rosecrown
Sedum rhodanthum

pink

A
S
M

wet soil

Flowers deep red, in flat-topped cluster,
Kingscrown
Sedum integrifolium

deep red

A S

wet soi

PEA FAMILY *(Fabaceae* or *Leguminosae)* Large family with compound leaves, pea or bean-like fruits. Flower irregular with typical pea shape (see illus. p 69). Stamens ten, partly united. Ovary superior. Leaves alternate.

Leaflets more than three; flowers usually not yellow, next page.

Leaflets three, flowers arranged

- in heads, pink, purple or white,
  Clover
  Trifolium sp.
  Native, leafless stems: *T. dasyphyllum, T. parryi,* illus. Introduced with leafy stems: *T. hybridum, T. pratense, T. repens.*
- in racemes, yellow or white; flowers are
  - tiny (less than ¼ in. long), fragrant,
    Sweetclover
    Melilotus officinalis
    M. alba, flowers white.
  - large, not fragrant,
    Golden Banner
    Thermopsis sp.
    T. divaricarpa, illus.; *T. montana.*

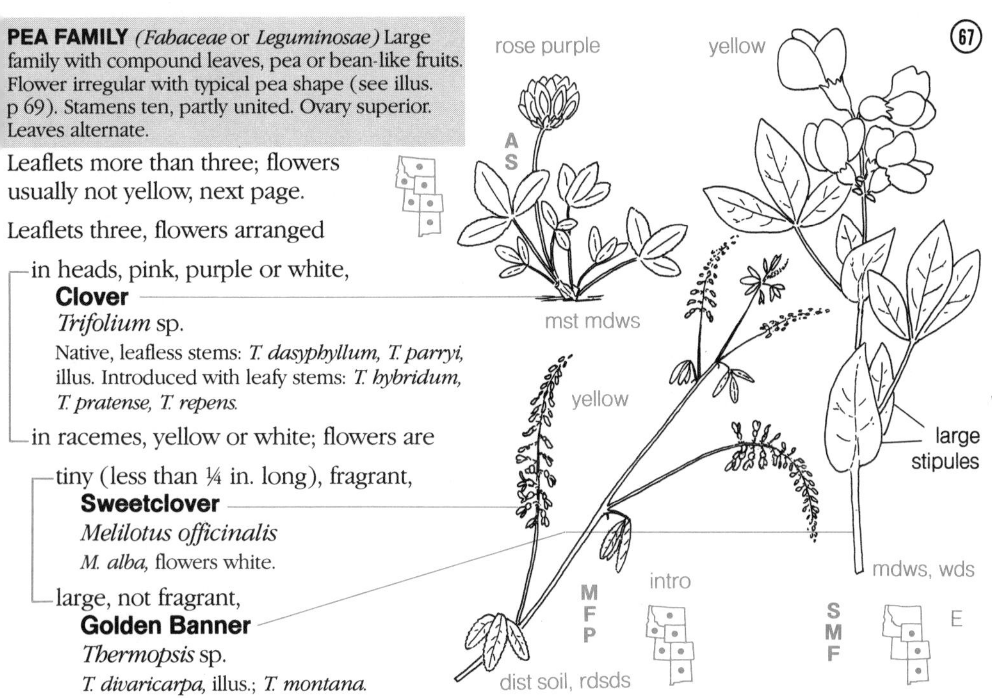
rose purple
A
S
mst mdws
yellow
yellow
M
F
P
intro
dist soil, rdsds
large stipules
mdws, wds
S
M
F
E

 Pea (from p67)

Leaves palmately compound

Lupine

Lupinus argenteus

L. parviflorus, L. plattensis, L. sericeus, others.

Leaves pinnately compound; tendrils are

- absent; flowers
  - not in umbels, next page.
  - in umbels,

    Crown Vetch

    Coronilla varia
- present; style has
  - hairs along one side like a toothbrush,

    White Pea Vine

    Lathyrus leucanthus
  - a tuft of hair at tip,

Climbing Vetch

Vicia americana

V. villosa (Hairy Vetch), soft hairy plant with long racemes.

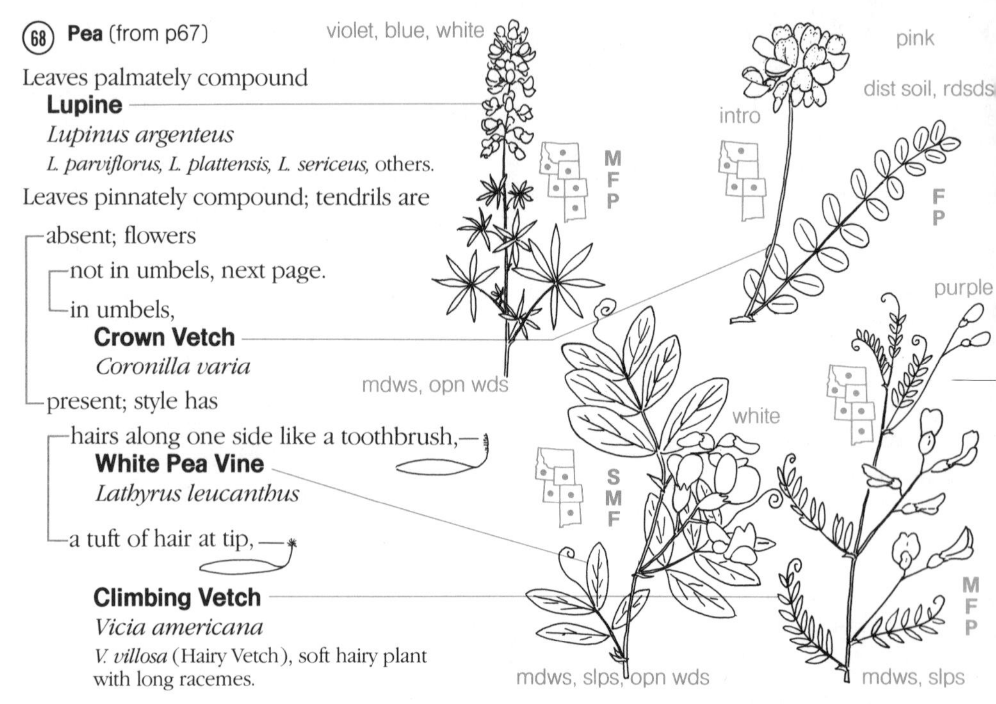
violet, blue, white
M
F
P
mdws, opn wds
pink
dist soil, rdsds
intro
F
P
purple
white
S
M
F
mdws, slps, opn wds
M
F
P
mdws, slps

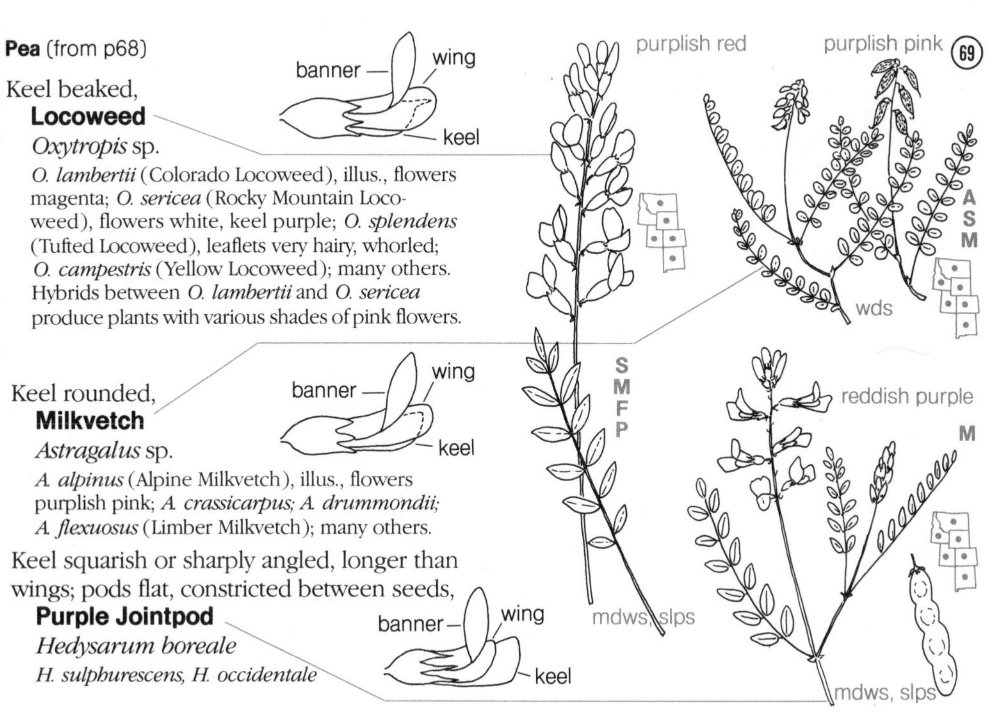
banner
wing
keel
purplish red
purplish pink
A
S
M
wds
S
M
F
P
mdws, slps
banner
wing
keel
reddish purple
M
banner
wing
keel
mdws, slps

Pea (from p68)

Keel beaked,
Locoweed
Oxytropis sp.

O. lambertii (Colorado Locoweed), illus., flowers magenta; *O. sericea* (Rocky Mountain Locoweed), flowers white, keel purple; *O. splendens* (Tufted Locoweed), leaflets very hairy, whorled; *O. campestris* (Yellow Locoweed); many others. Hybrids between *O. lambertii* and *O. sericea* produce plants with various shades of pink flowers.

Keel rounded,
Milkvetch
Astragalus sp.

A. alpinus (Alpine Milkvetch), illus., flowers purplish pink; *A. crassicarpus; A. drummondii; A. flexuosus* (Limber Milkvetch); many others.

Keel squarish or sharply angled, longer than wings; pods flat, constricted between seeds,
Purple Jointpod
Hedysarum boreale
H. sulphurescens, H. occidentale

FUMITORY FAMILY *(Fumariaceae)* Herbs with smooth, divided compound leaves. Flowers irregular, spurred. Four petals, two united at tip.

Golden Smoke

Corydalis aurea

C. caseana, flowers pink.

GENTIAN FAMILY *(Gentianaceae)* Herbs with simple entire leaves which are opposite or whorled. Flowers regular with four or five united petals.

Petals clearly united, next page.

Petals appear separate; flowers are

- dull purple or blue,
  Star Gentian
  Swertia perennis
- white, greenish or blue-tinged; plant is
  - over 1ft tall,
    Monument Plant
    Frasera speciosa
  - shorter,
    Marsh Felwort
    Lomatogonium rotatum

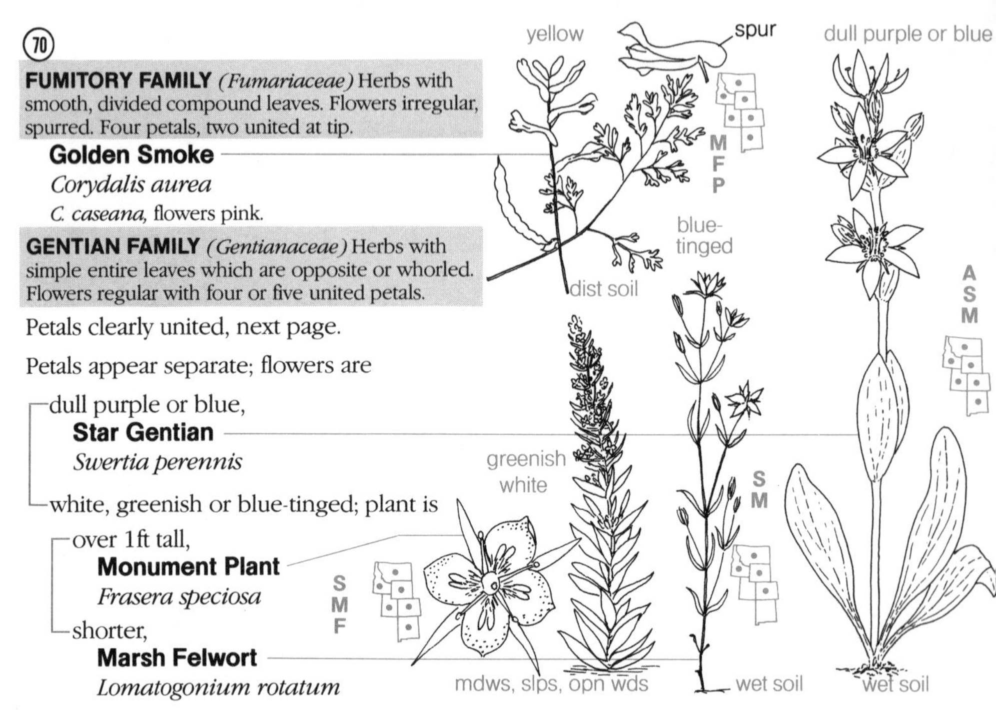
yellow
spur
M F P
dist soil
dull purple or blue
A S M
wet soil
blue-tinged
S M
wet soil
greenish white
mdws, slps, opn wds
S M F

Gentian (from p70)

Flowers with fringe of hairs in throat,
Rose Gentian
Gentianella amarella

Flowers not as above; petals are

- blue or purplish, next page.
- white with blue or green streaks, blotches,
  Arctic Gentian
  Gentiana algida

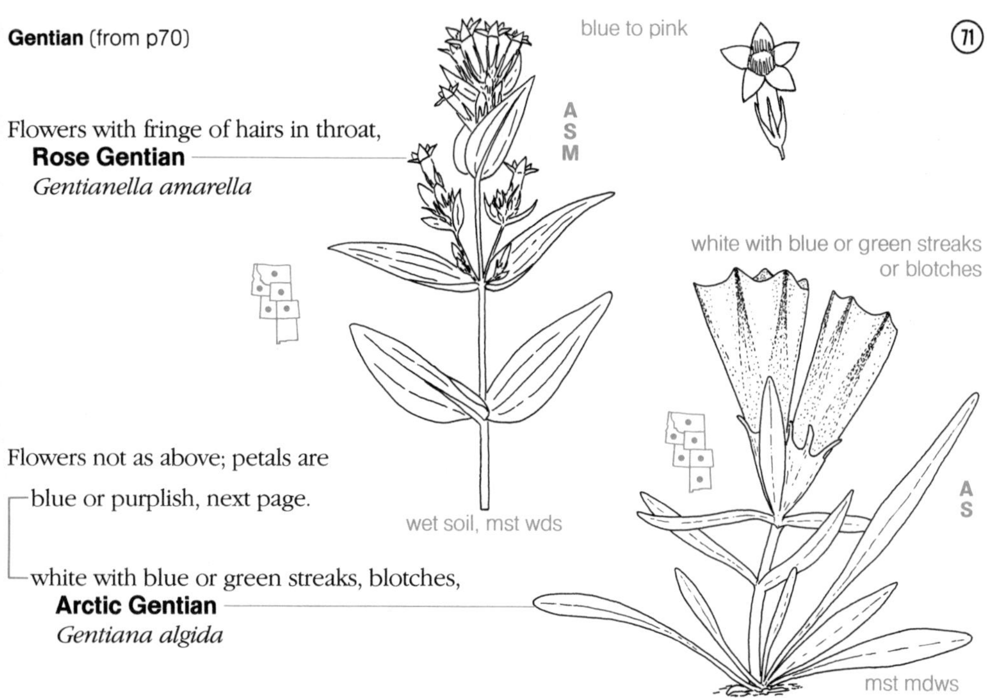
blue to pink
A
S
M
wet soil, mst wds
white with blue or green streaks
or blotches
A
S
mst mdws

Gentian (from p71)

Corolla four-lobed; flowers are

- subtended by two bract-like leaves, **Fragrant Gentian** *Gentianopsis barbellata*
- without bract-like leaves, **Rocky Mountain Fringed Gentian** *Gentianopsis thermalis*

Corolla five-lobed; upper leaves are

- narrow; flowers less than 1in long, **Rocky Mountain Gentian** *Gentiana affinis*
- broad; flowers larger, **Parry Gentian** *Gentiana calycosa*

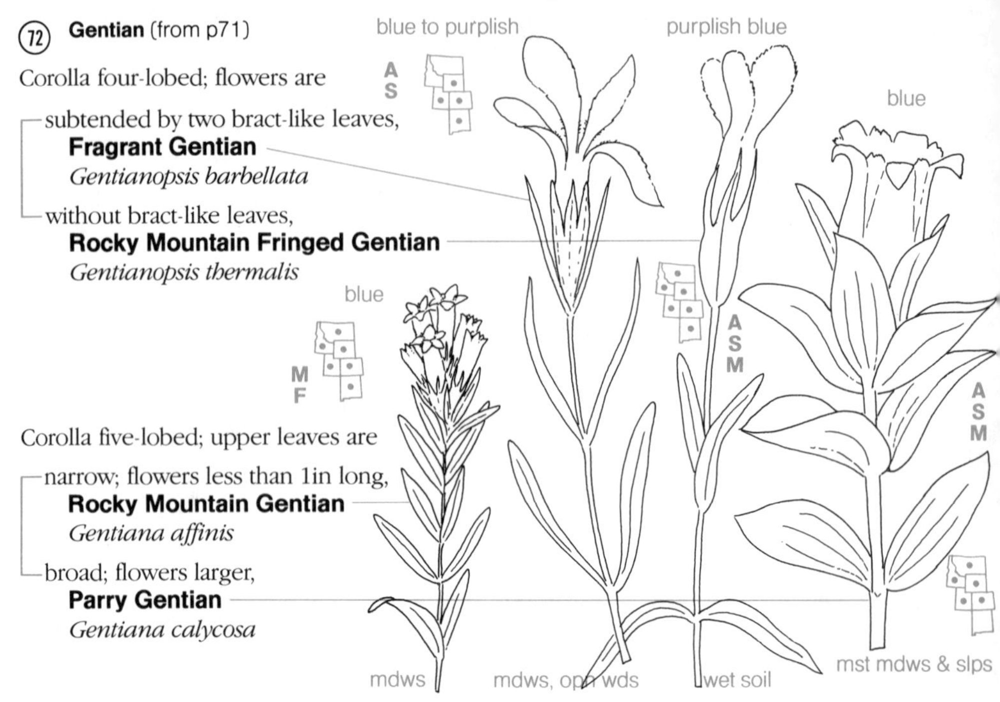
blue to purplish
A
S
purplish blue
blue
A
S
M
blue
M
F
A
S
M
mdws
mdws, op wds
wet soil
mst mdws & slps

GERANIUM FAMILY *(Geraniaceae)* Flowers regular with five separate petals, five or ten stamens, superior ovary topped with a style that forms a long beak. Leaves palmately lobed or pinnately compound.

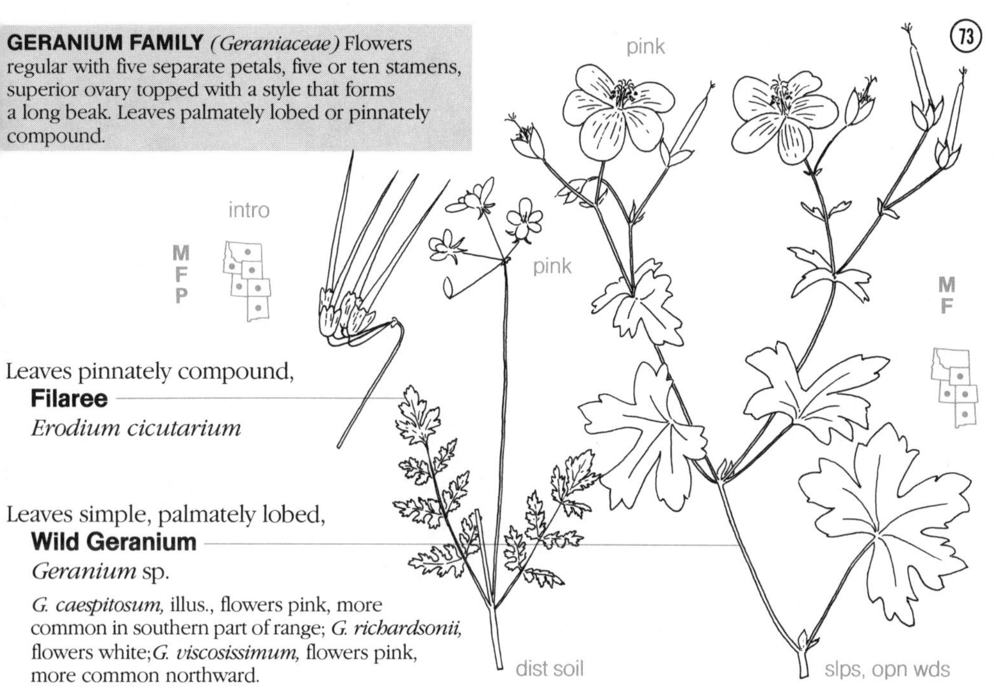
pink
intro
M
F
P
pink
M
F
dist soil
slps, opn wds

Leaves pinnately compound,
Filaree
Erodium cicutarium

Leaves simple, palmately lobed,
Wild Geranium
Geranium sp.

G. caespitosum, illus., flowers pink, more common in southern part of range; *G. richardsonii,* flowers white; *G. viscosissimum,* flowers pink, more common northward.

WATERLEAF FAMILY *(Hydrophyllaceae)* Flowers often in coiled clusters with stamens often extending beyond the petals. Flowers regular, with five united petals, five stamens, superior ovary.

Flowers in a single spike-like inflorescence,

Purple Fringe
Phacelia sericea

Flowers not as above; leaves

—composed of large, thin leaflets,

Fendler Waterleaf
Hydrophyllum fendleri

H. capitatum (Ballhead Waterleaf), flowers lavender, overtopped by leaves.

—not as above; plant may be sticky,

Scorpion Weed
Phacelia sp.

P. alba, illus.; *P. glandulosa,* flowers purple to blue-violet, leaves pinnately compound; *P. hastata,* flowers lavender, leaves simple, not lobed; *P. heterophylla,* flowers white, leaves simple with basal leaves lobed; *Phacelia linearis* (Narrow-leaved Phacelia), annual, flowers blue-lavender, leaves simple, entire or with few lobes.

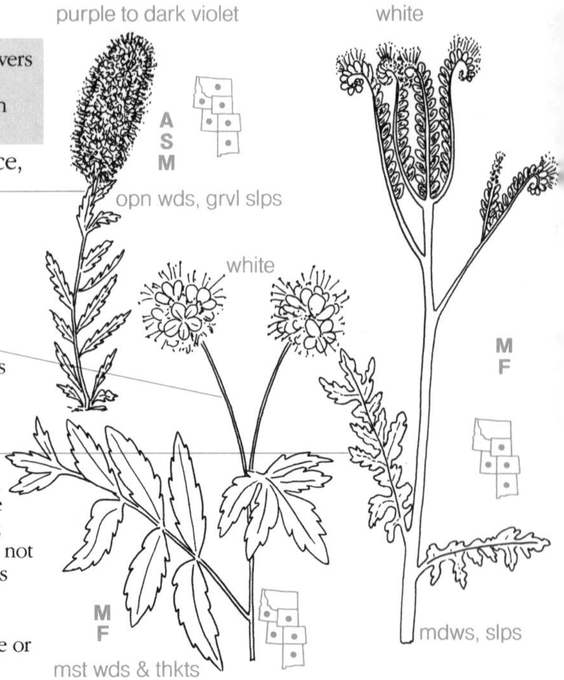

purple to dark violet

A
S
M

opn wds, grvl slps

white

M
F

mst wds & thkts

white

M
F

mdws, slps

ST. JOHNSWORT FAMILY *(Hypericaceae)*
Flowers regular with five separate yellow or orange petals, many stamens. Ovary superior. Leaves entire, opposite, with translucent dots.

Flowers many,
Klamath Weed
Hypericum perforatum

Flowers few,
St. Johnswort
Hypericum formosus

IRIS FAMILY *(Iridaceae)* Flowers regular with three petal-like sepals, three petals, three stamens, inferior ovary. Leaves long, narrow with overlapping bases.

Flowers resemble garden iris,
Rocky Mountain Iris
Iris missouriensis

Flowers not as above,
Blue-eyed Grass
Sisyrinchium montanum

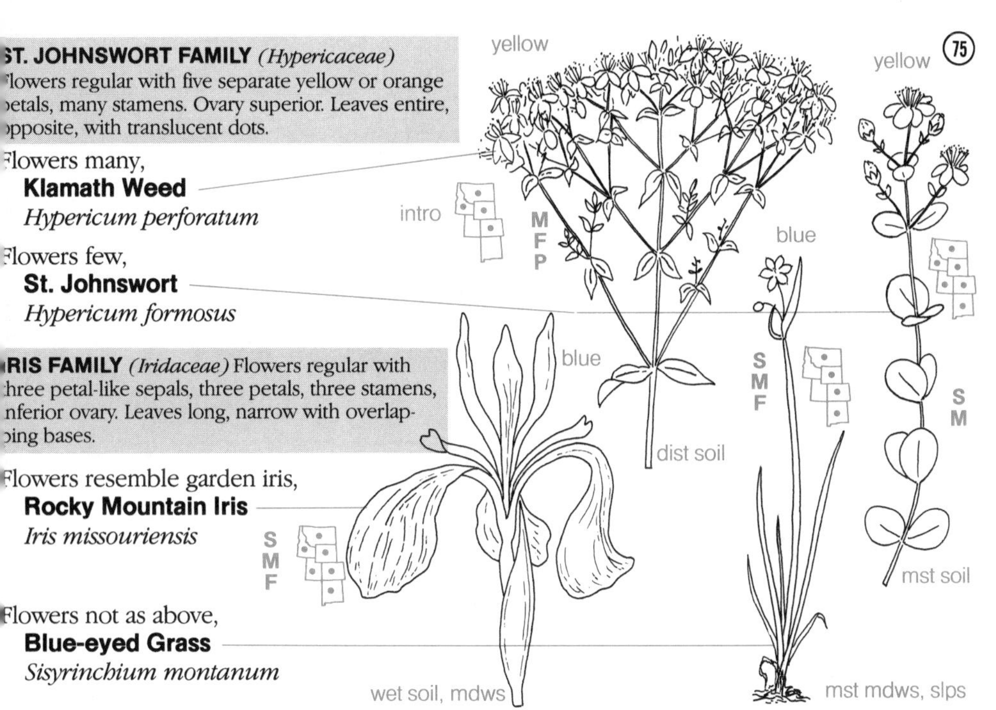
yellow
intro
M
F
P
dist soil
yellow
S
M
mst soil
blue
S
M
F
wet soil, mdws
blue
S
M
F
mst mdws, slps

MINT FAMILY *(Lamiaceae* or *Labiatae)* Mostly aromatic herbs with irregular two-lipped flowers with five united petals. Stems square with simple, opposite leaves. Stamens two or four, ovary superior with four lobes maturing into four nutlets.

Flowers in dense clusters in leaf axils, next page.

Flowers one to few in leaf axils, p78.

Flowers in heads,
Horsemint
Monarda fistulosa

Flowers in spikes which are
- spiny,
  Dragonhead
  Moldavica parviflora
- not spiny; stamens
  - extend beyond petals,
    Giant Hyssop
    Agastache urticifolia
  - not as above,
    Prunella
    Prunella vulgaris

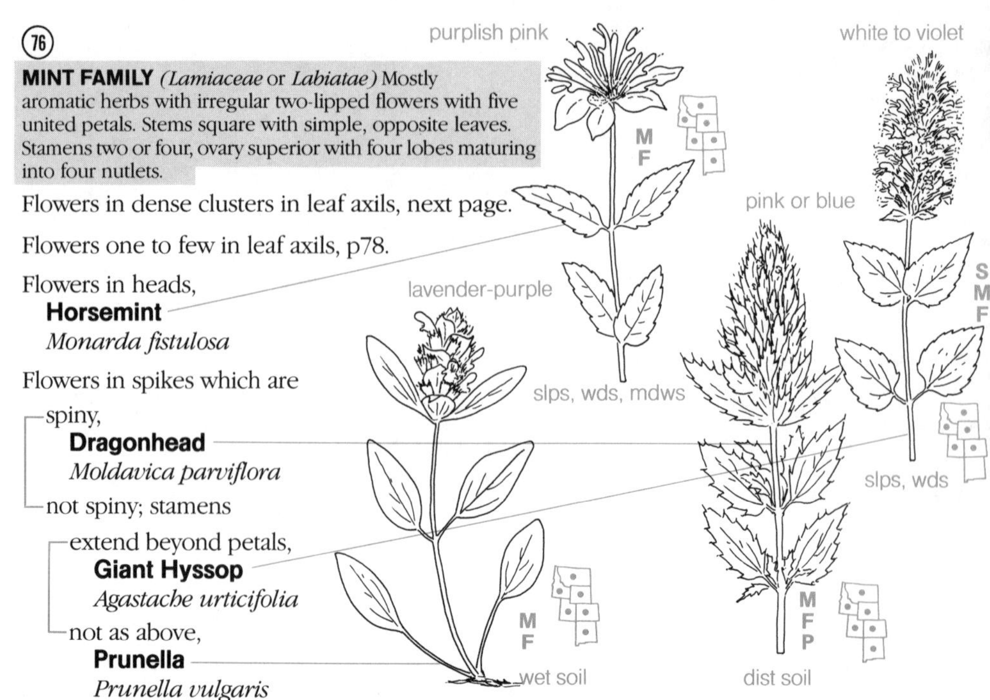
purplish pink
M
F
slps, wds, mdws
white to violet
S
M
F
slps, wds
pink or blue
M
F
P
dist soil
lavender-purple
M
F
wet soil

Mint (from p76)

Plant woolly hairy,
Common Horehound
Marrubium vulgare

Plant not as above; calyx teeth are

—bristle-like, flowers large,
Whorled Monarda
Monarda pectinata

—not as above, flowers tiny,
Wild Mint
Mentha arvensis

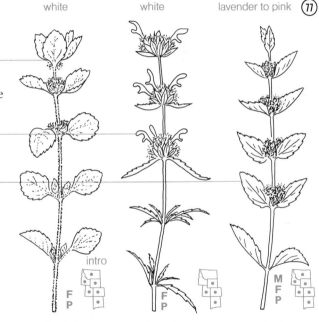

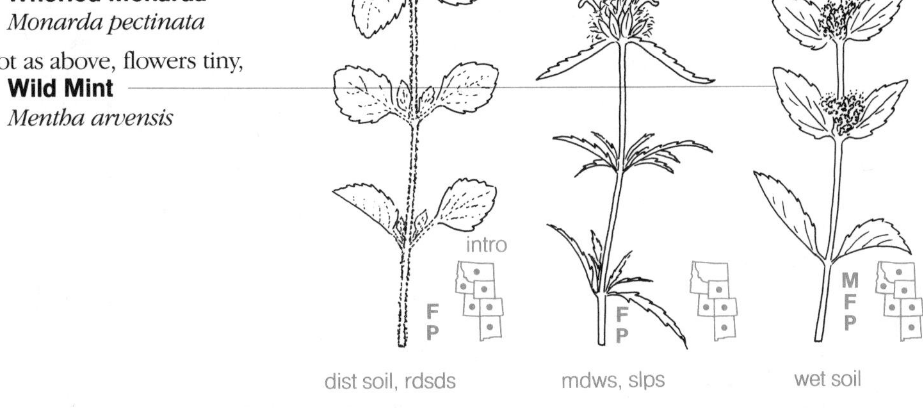
white
white
lavender to pink
intro
F
P
F
P
M
F
P
dist soil, rdsds
mdws, slps
wet soil

 Mint (from p76)

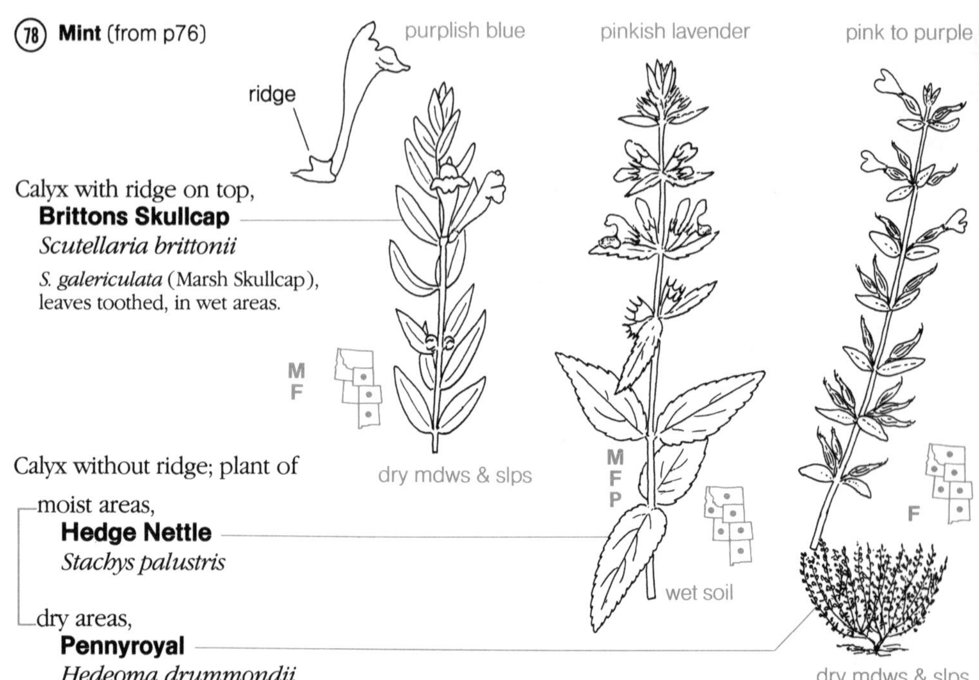
ridge
purplish blue
pinkish lavender
pink to purple
M
F
dry mdws & slps
M
F
P
wet soil
F
dry mdws & slps

Calyx with ridge on top,
Brittons Skullcap
Scutellaria brittonii
S. galericulata (Marsh Skullcap), leaves toothed, in wet areas.

Calyx without ridge; plant of

- moist areas,
  Hedge Nettle
  Stachys palustris
- dry areas,
  Pennyroyal
  Hedeoma drummondii

LADDERWORT FAMILY *(Lentibulariaceae)*
quatic plants whose finely divided leaves have adders which trap and digest insects. Irregular owers with two sepals, a spur.

Common Bladderwort
Utricularia vulgaris

LILY FAMILY *(Liliaceae)* Regular flowers with ree usually petal-like sepals, three petals, usually x stamens, superior ovary.

etals appear to be six (sepals petal-like), ext page.

etals three; leaves are

- three broad, whorled,
  Western Trillium
  Trillium ovatum

- not as above,
  Mariposa Lily
  Calochortus sp.
  C. elegans, C. gunnisonii, illus., *C. nuttallii,* others.

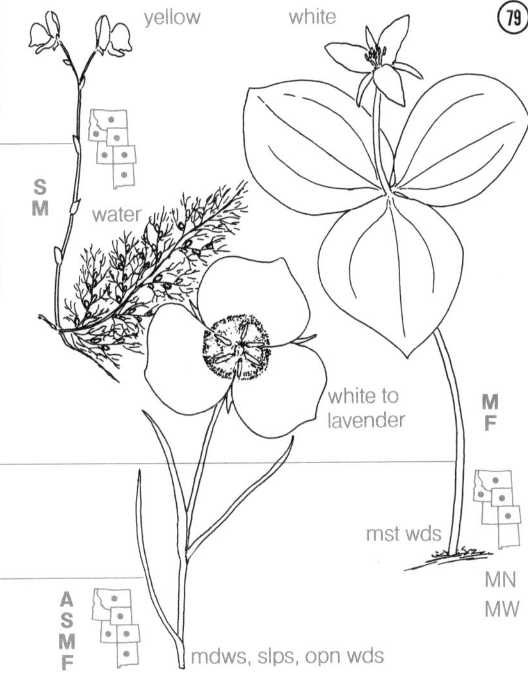
yellow
white
S
M
water
white to
lavender
M
F
mst wds
MN
MW
A
S
M
F
mdws, slps, opn wds

 Lily (from p79)

Flowers yellow or orange-red, next page.

Flowers white, pink, greenish or yellowish, p82.

Flowers brown or purple, spotted with yellow or white,

Purple Fritillaria
Fritillaria atropurpurea

Flowers blue, arranged in

- umbel,
  Wild Hyacinth
  Triteleia grandiflora
- raceme,
  Common Camas
  Camassia quamash

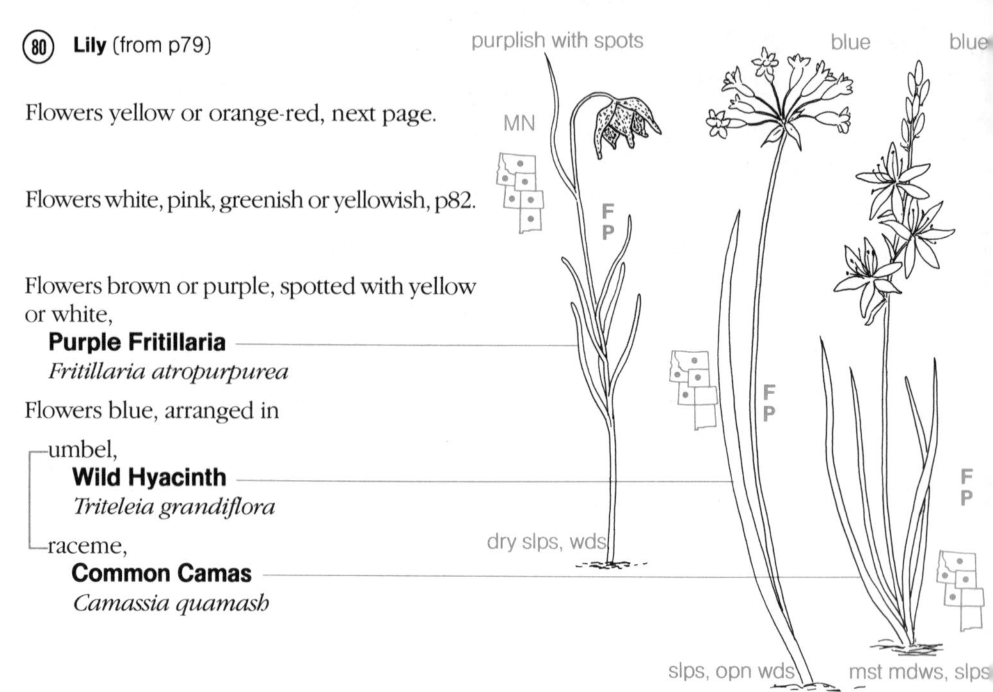
purplish with spots
MN
F
P
dry slps, wds
blue
F
P
slps, opn wds
blue
F
P
mst mdws, slps

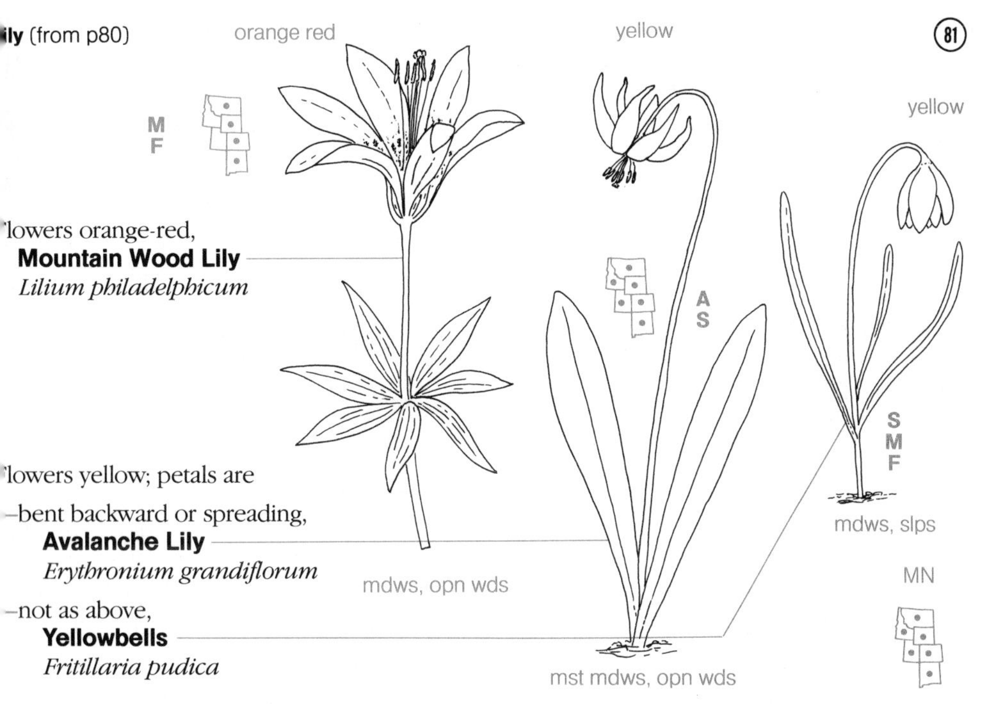
orange red
yellow
yellow
M
F
A
S
S
M
F
mdws, opn wds
mst mdws, opn wds
mdws, slps
MN

lowers orange-red,
Mountain Wood Lily
Lilium philadelphicum

lowers yellow; petals are

–bent backward or spreading,
Avalanche Lily
Erythronium grandiflorum

–not as above,
Yellowbells
Fritillaria pudica

(82) **Lily** (from p80)

Leaves neither long and narrow nor wide and pleated, p84.

Leaves wide, pleated,

Corn Husk Lily

Veratrum californicum

V. viride, flowers green or yellowish green, MT,ID.

Leaves long, narrow, grass-like; stem is

- absent,

  Sandlily

  Leucocrinum montanum

- present; plant has

  - no onion odor, next page.
  - onion odor when crushed; flowers in umbel,

    Wild Onion

    Allium sp.

    A. geyeri, illus.; *A. cernuum* (Nodding Onion), flowers pink, umbel nodding; *A. textile* (Sand Onion), flowers white; *A. brevistylum; A. schoenoprasum; A. acuminatum;* others.

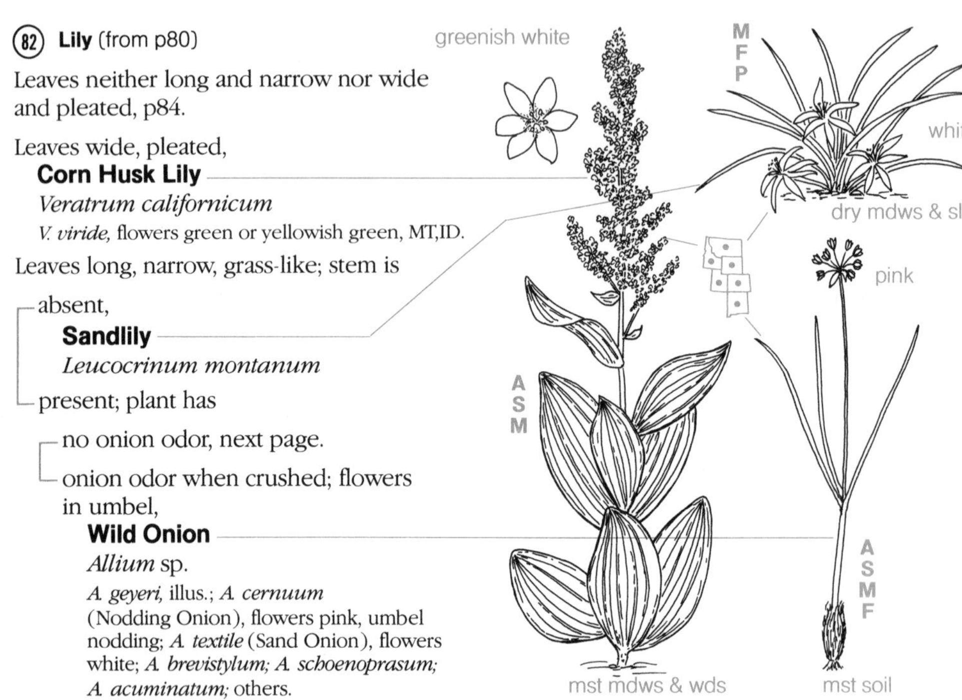
greenish white
M
F
P
white
dry mdws & slp
pink
A
S
M
A
S
M
F
mst mdws & wds
mst soil

Lily (from p82)

Stem stout; leaves tough, wiry,
Beargrass
Xerophyllum tenax

Stem and leaves not as above; flowers are

- in clusters of twos or threes,
  Tofieldia
  Tofieldia glutinosa ssp. *montana*
- not as above,
  Death Camas
  Zigadenus sp.
  Z. elegans, petals over ¼ in. long, moist areas;
  Z. venenosus, illus., petals smaller, dry areas.

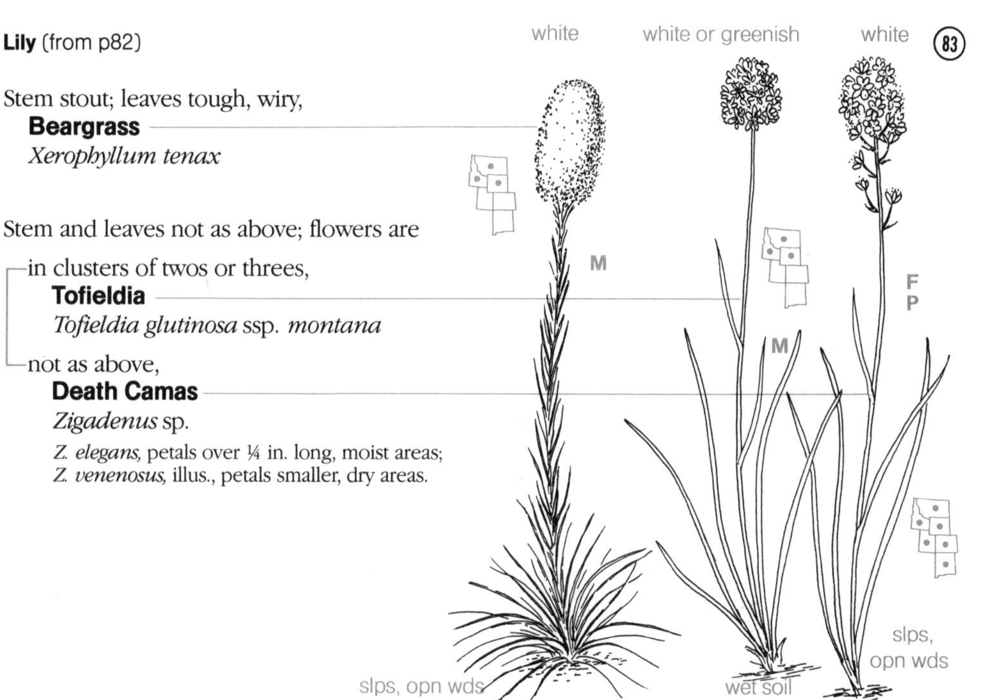
white
white or greenish
white
M
M
F
P
slps, opn wds
wet soil
slps, opn wds

 Lily (from p82)

Flowers in leaf axils,
Twisted-stalk
Streptopus amplexifolius

Flowers terminal on stem, with

one flower per stalk,
Queenscup
Clintonia uniflora

several flowers per stalk,
Solomonplume
Smilacina sp.
S. stellata, illus., flowers few; *S. racemosa,* flowers numerous.

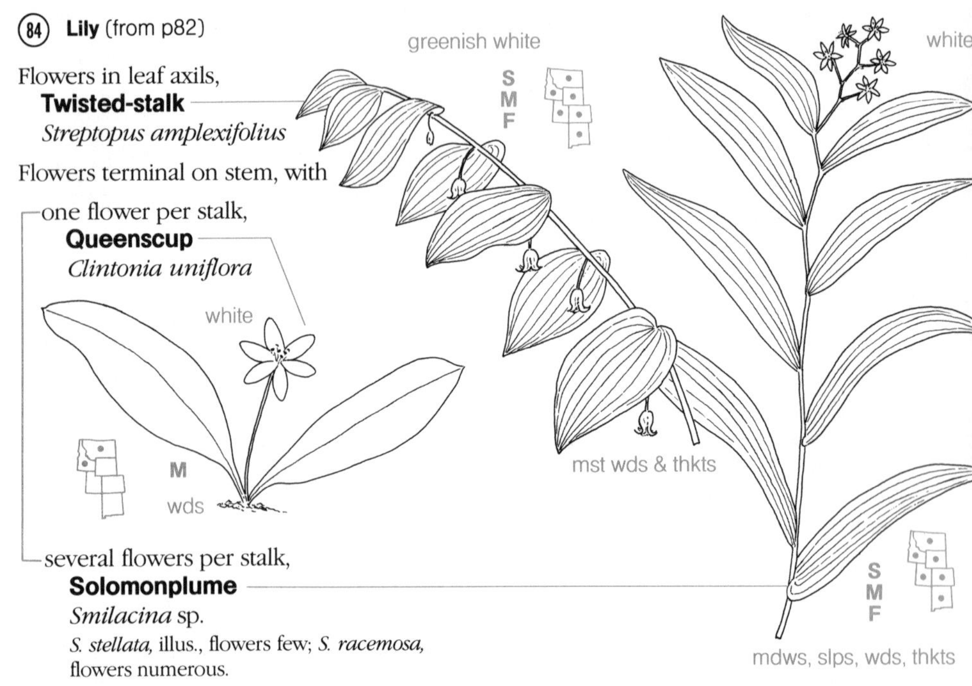
greenish white
S
M
F
mst wds & thkts
white
M
wds
white
S
M
F
mdws, slps, wds, thkts

FLAX FAMILY *(Linaceae)*

FLAX FAMILY *(Linaceae)* Regular flowers with five separate petals and sepals, five stamens, superior ovary. Petals fall easily. Leaves alternate, narrow.

Blue Flax

Linum lewisii

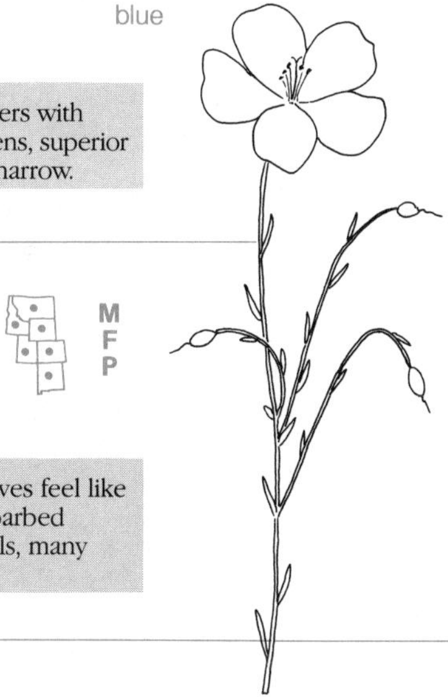

blue

M
F
P

dry mdws

STICK-LEAF FAMILY *(Loasaceae)*

STICK-LEAF FAMILY *(Loasaceae)* Leaves feel like sandpaper, stick to clothing due to tiny barbed hairs. Regular flowers with separate petals, many stamens, inferior ovary.

Evening Star

Mentzelia sp.

Flowers white or cream: *M. decapetala* (Giant Evening Star), illus., petals over 2in long; *M. nuda,* petals smaller. Flowers yellow: *M. albicaulis, M. multiflora, M. laevicaulis, M. speciosa,* others.

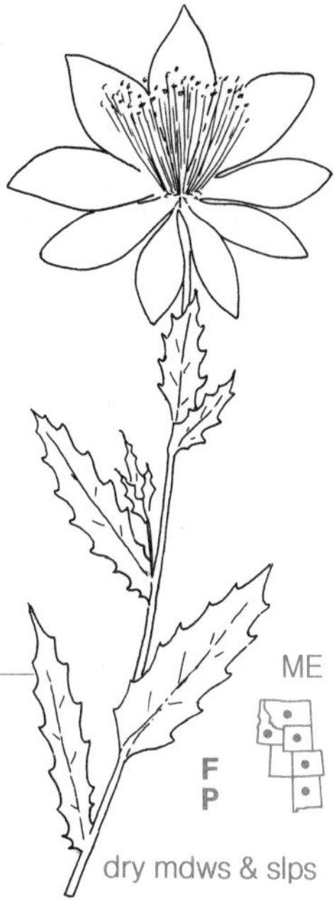

white or cream

ME
F
P

dry mdws & slps

MALLOW FAMILY *(Malvaceae)* Regular flowers with five petals, many stamens forming a tube. Ovary superior, often resembles a cheese wheel. Leaves palmately veined.

Leaves maple-like,

Mountain Hollyhock
Iliamna rivularis

Leaves not maple-like; flowers are

—orange,

Scarlet Mallow
Cowboys Delight
Sphaeralcea coccinea
S. monroana (Monroe Globemallow), leaves with shallow lobes, MT, WY, UT, ID.

—white,

Modest Mallow
Sidalcea candida

—rose-purple,

Wild Hollyhock
Sidalcea neomexicana

white or pinkish to rose purple
MW
S
M
mdws, wds, wet soil
orange
F
P
dry mdws, rdsds
white
S
M
F
wet soil
rose-purple
M
F
mst mdws

FOUR-O'CLOCK FAMILY *(Nyctaginaceae)* Regular flowers subtended by separate or united bracts. Petals absent, sepals petal-like, united. Leaves opposite.

Bracts cup-like,
Showy Four-O'Clock
Mirabilis multiflora

Bracts not as above,
Wild Four-O'Clock
Oxybaphus sp.
O. hirsutus, O. linearis, illus.

WATERLILY FAMILY *(Nymphaeaceae)* Aquatic plants with large showy flowers. Flowers regular, with sepals grading into petals. Stamens many.

Yellow Waterlily
Nuphar luteum ssp. *polysepalum*

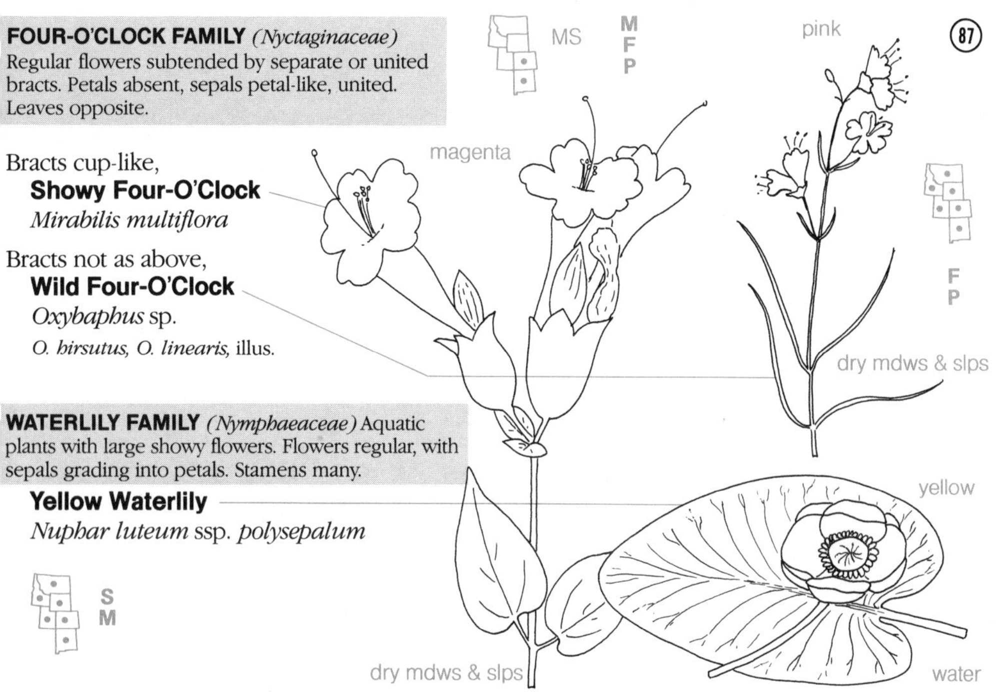
MS
M
F
P
pink
magenta
F
P
dry mdws & slps
yellow
S
M
dry mdws & slps
water

EVENING PRIMROSE FAMILY *(Onagraceae)*
Regular flowers with four separate petals (floral tube may be present), four sepals, eight stamens, inferior ovary.

Flowers less than 1/3 in. wide,

Willowherb
Epilobium sp.
E. ciliatum, E. hornemannii, illus., others.

Flowers wider, and

- pink, dark pink, magenta, next page.
- yellow, p90
- bright red,
  Hummingbird Trumpet
  Zauschneria latifolia var. *garrettii*
- white,
  Evening Primrose
  Oenothera sp.
  O. coronopifolia (Cut-leaf Evening Primrose), petals less than ½ in. long; *O. albicaulis,* petals more than ½ in. long, leaves pinnately dissected; *O. caespitosa,* illus., stemless; *O. nuttallii;* others.

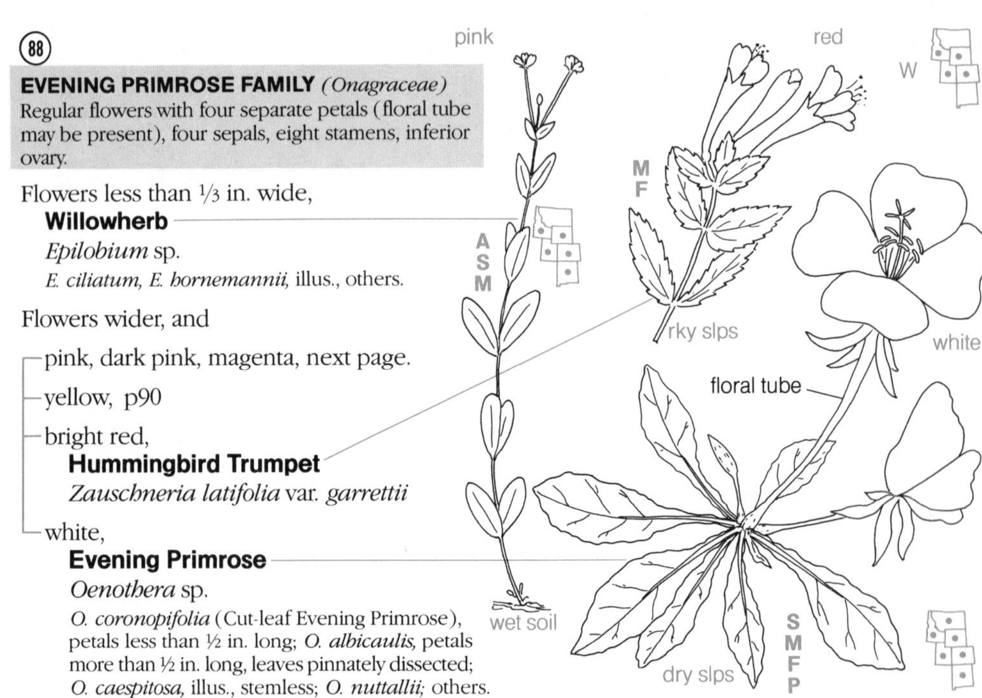
pink
A
S
M
wet soil
red
W
M
F
rky slps
white
floral tube
S
M
F
P
dry slps

Evening Primrose (from p88)

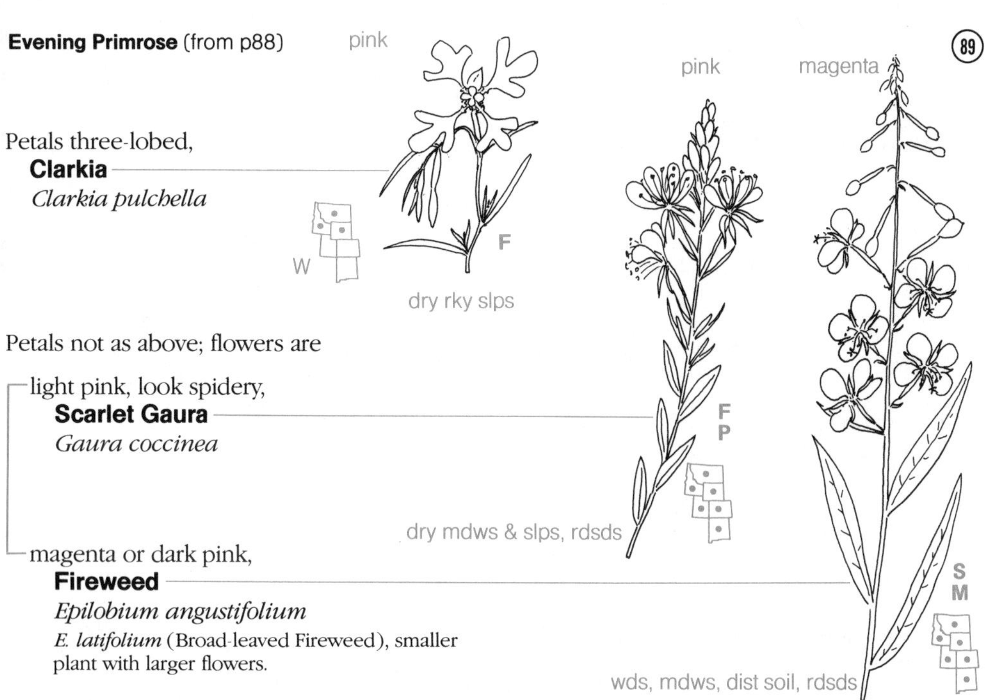
pink
F
W
dry rky slps
pink
F
P
dry mdws & slps, rdsds
magenta
S
M
wds, mdws, dist soil, rdsds

Petals three-lobed,
Clarkia
Clarkia pulchella

Petals not as above; flowers are

- light pink, look spidery,
  Scarlet Gaura
  Gaura coccinea
- magenta or dark pink,
  Fireweed
  Epilobium angustifolium
  E. latifolium (Broad-leaved Fireweed), smaller plant with larger flowers.

Evening Primrose (from p88)

Plant with many stems,
Dainty Sundrops
Calylophus serrulata

Plant with one main stem,
Yellow Evening Primrose
Oenothera villosa var. *strigosa*
O. hookeri, flower over 2in wide.

Plant stemless,
Yellow Stemless Evening Primrose
Oenothera brachycarpa
O. flava, petals less than 1in long, leaves pinnately lobed.

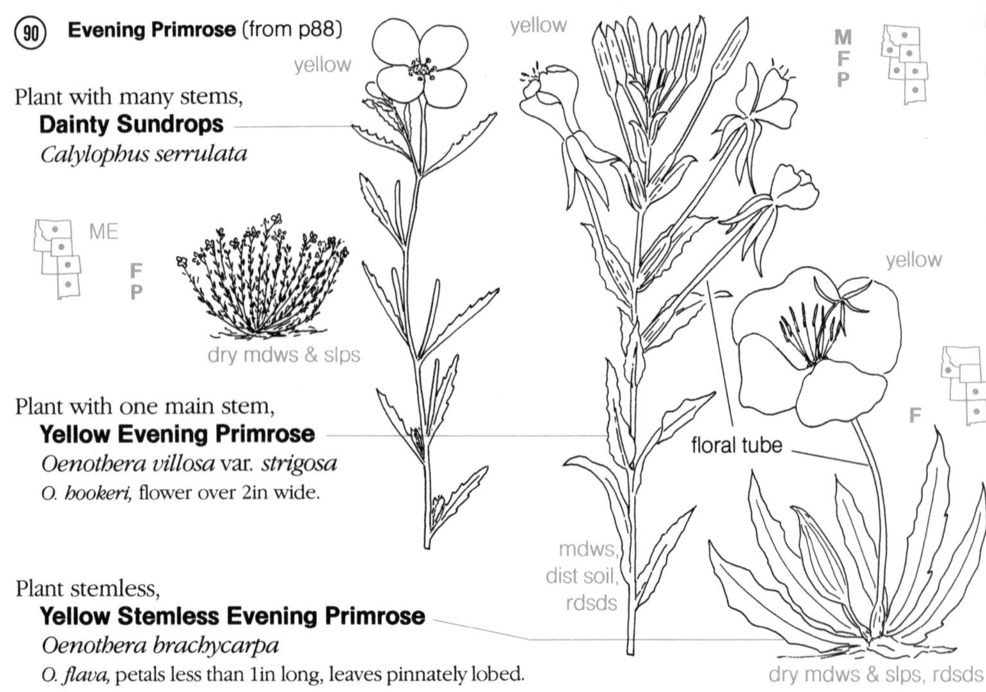
yellow
ME
F
P
dry mdws & slps
yellow
M
F
P
mdws,
dist soil,
rdsds
yellow
floral tube
F
dry mdws & slps, rdsds

ORCHID FAMILY *(Orchidaceae)* Irregular flowers with three petals, the lower petal forming a sac or lip, three petal-like sepals. Stamens and pistil united into a column, ovary inferior. Leaves simple.

Plant not green (lacks chlorophyll),

Coralroot *Corallorhiza* sp.

C. maculata (Spotted Coralroot), illus.; *C. trifida* (Little Yellow Coralroot); *C. striata* (Striped Coralroot); *C. wisteriana* (Spring Coralroot).

Plant with green leaves; flowers are

- yellow, dull purplish to brownish,

  Lady Slipper *Cypripedium* sp.

  C. calceolus, illus., *C. fasciculatum, C. montanum.* (All rare and endangered.)

- rose-purple,

  Fairy Slipper, Calypso

  Calypso bulbosa

- white or greenish; leaves

  - entirely green, next page.
  - with white markings,

    Western Rattlesnake-plantain

    Goodyera oblongifolia

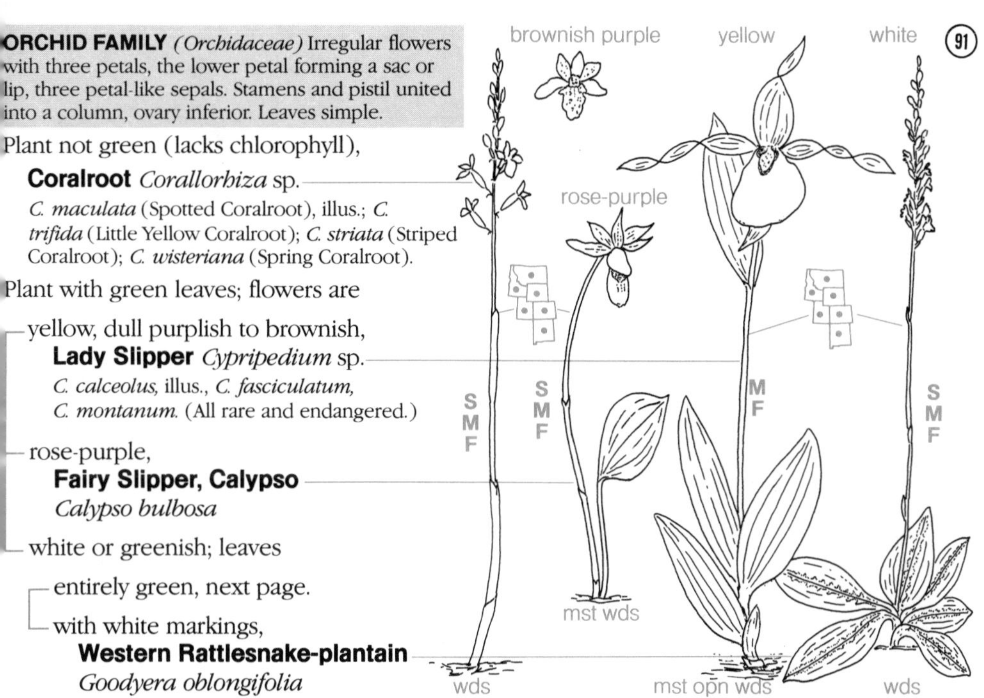

brownish purple
yellow
white
rose-purple
S M F
S M F
M F
S M F
mst wds
wds
mst opn wds
wds

(92) **Orchid** (from p91)

Stem with one leaf,

One-leaved Orchid
Platanthera obtusata

Stem with two leaves, which are

- basal,
  Two-leaved Wood Orchid
  Platanthera orbiculata
- midway up stem,
  Heart-leaved Twayblade
  Listera cordata

Stem with more than two leaves; spike is

- twisted,
  Ladies-tresses
  Spiranthes romanzoffiana
- not twisted,
  Bog-orchid
  Coeloglossum viride var. *virescens,* illus.
  Platanthera sp.
  Platanthera dilatata (White Bog-orchid);
  P. hyperborea (Northern Green Bog-orchid), bracts short.

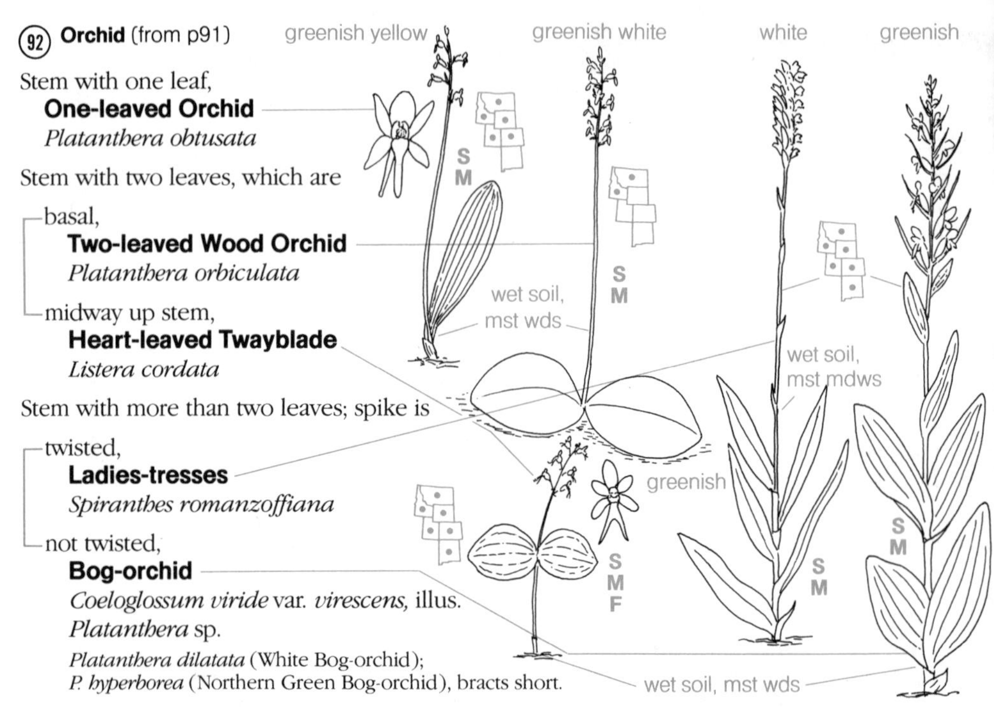
greenish yellow
S
M
greenish white
S
M
wet soil,
mst wds
white
wet soil,
mst mdws
greenish
greenish
S
M
F
S
M
S
M
wet soil, mst wds

ROOMRAPE FAMILY *(Orobanchaceae)* Parasitic on-green plants with irregular flowers which semble the Figwort Family. Petals five, united. vary superior.

Broomrape
Orobanche fasciculata
O. uniflora, short main stem.

OOD SORREL FAMILY *(Oxalidaceae)* Herbs ith regular flowers, superior ovary, ten stamens. aves compound. Juice contains sour oxalic acid.

Yellow Wood Sorrel
Oxalis dillenii

OPPY FAMILY *(Papaveraceae)* Regular flowers ith four to six separate petals. Sepals 2 (3), fall rly. Stamens many, ovary superior. Juice yellowish milky.

Pricklypoppy
Argemone polyanthemos

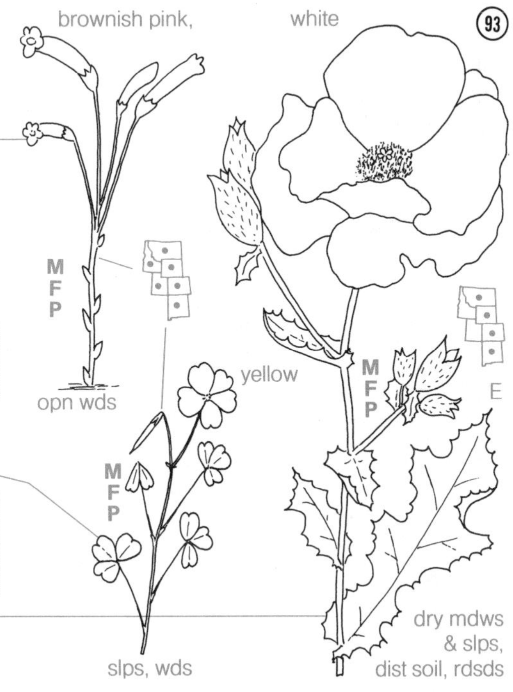
brownish pink,
white
M
F
P
opn wds
yellow
M
F
P
E
M
F
P
slps, wds
dry mdws
& slps,
dist soil, rdsds

PHLOX FAMILY *(Polemoniaceae)* Regular flowers with five united petals, superior ovary. Stigma usually three-lobed.

Leaves pinnately compound, next page.

Leaves palmately compound, appear whorled,

Nuttall Gilia

Linanthastrum nuttallii

Leaves simple; flowers,

- in a dense spike-like inflorescence,

  Spike Gilia

  Ipomopsis spicata

- in a head,

  Collomia

  Collomia linearis

- not as above,

  Phlox

  Phlox sp.

  P. bryoides, P. hoodii, illus., *P. longifolia, P. multiflora,* others.

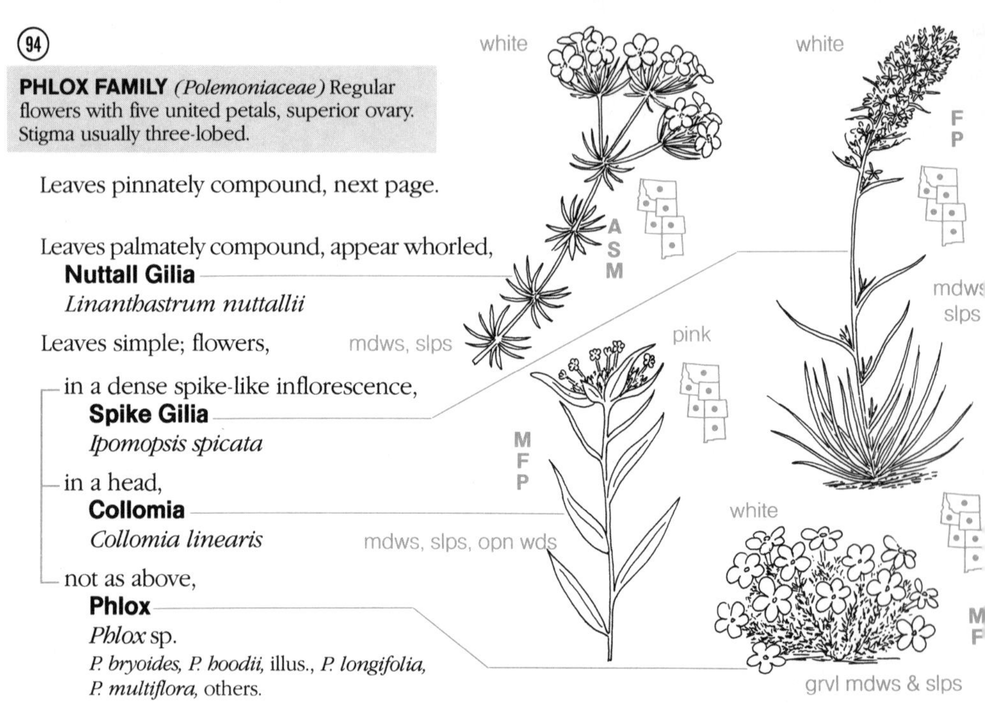
white
A
S
M
mdws, slps
white
F
P
mdws
slps
pink
M
F
P
mdws, slps, opn wds
white
M
F
grvl mdws & slps

hlox (from p94)

lowers blue to purplish, next page.

lowers white or cream-colored,
rranged in

- dense spike-like inflorescence,
  Spike Gilia
  Ipomopsis spicata
  (Illus. p94.)

- ball-like clusters,
  Ballhead Gilia
  Ipomopsis congesta

- not as above,
  White Fairy Trumpet
  Ipomopsis candida

lowers red,
Red Fairy Trumpet
Ipomopsis aggregata

lowers pink, hybrid between Red and
Vhite Fairy Trumpet.

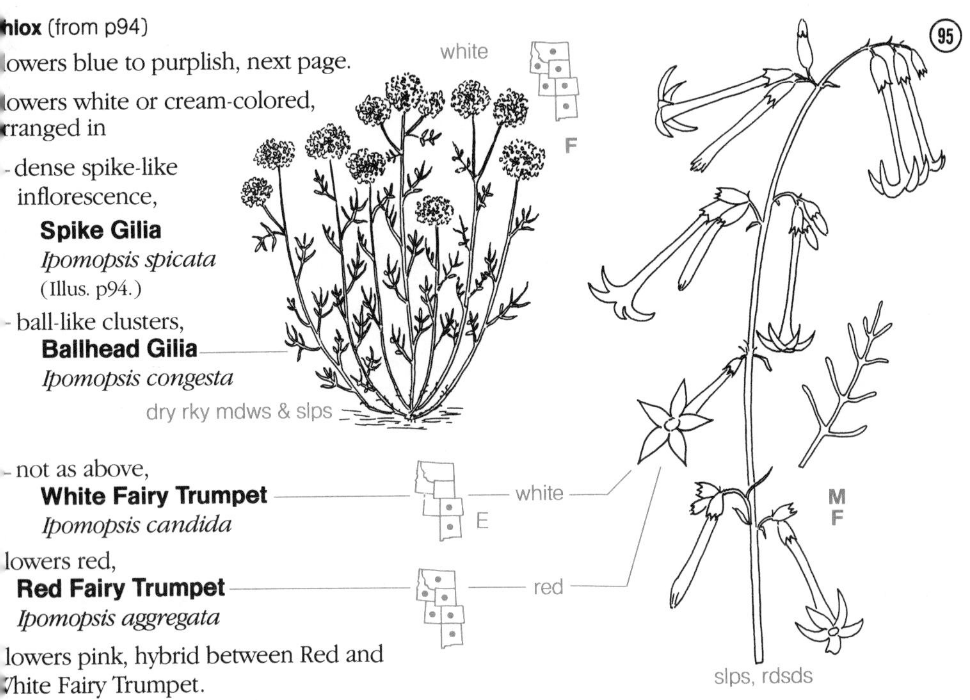
white
F
dry rky mdws & slps
white
E
red
M
F
slps, rdsds

96 **Phlox** (from p95)

Leaflets not whorled; flowers are

- tiny, shaped like this,
  Sticky Gilia
  Gilia pinnatifida

- not as above,
  Jacobs Ladder
  Polemonium sp.
  P. delicatum (Subalpine Jacobs Ladder), illus., under 6in tall; *P. caeruleum* (Western Jacobs Ladder), slender, unbranched, over 6in; *P. foliosissimum* (Leafy Jacobs Ladder), stout, branched.

Leaflets appear whorled,
Sky Pilot
Polemonium viscosum

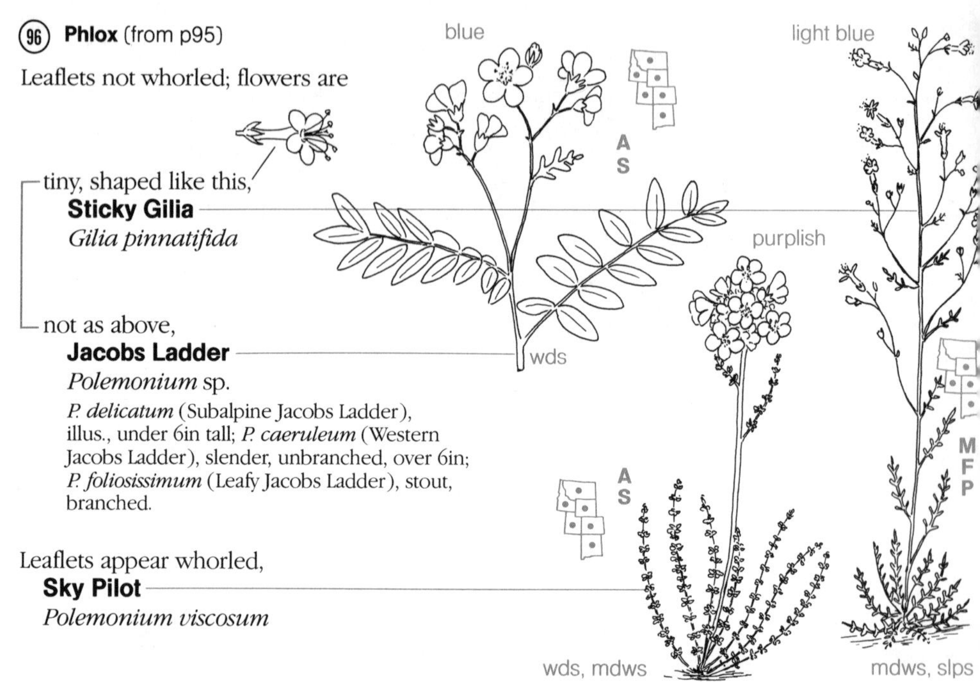

blue
A
S
wds
light blue
M
F
P
mdws, slps
purplish
A
S
wds, mdws

BUCKWHEAT FAMILY *(Polygonaceae)* Regular flowers with four, five or six perianth segments, superior ovary. Sheathing stipules present except in Eriogonum. Fruit often three-sided.

Leaves arrowhead shaped,

Sheep Sorrel

Rumex acetosella

Leaves woolly-hairy on underside,

Eriogonum

Eriogonum sp.

E. umbellatum (Sulfur Flower), illus.;
E. cernuum (Nodding Eriogonum); *E. flavum;*
E. jamesii; E. ovalifolium (Cushion Eriogonum);
E. subalpinum; others.

Leaves not as above, next page.

reddish
yellow
S
M
F
M
F
P
dist soil
dry mdws, slps

Buckwheat (from p97)

Flowers pink,
Water Buckwheat
Polygonum amphibium

Flowers white (or only tinged with pink)

—bulblets present on stem,
Alpine Bistort
Polygonum viviparum

—bulblets absent,
American Bistort
Polygonum bistortoides

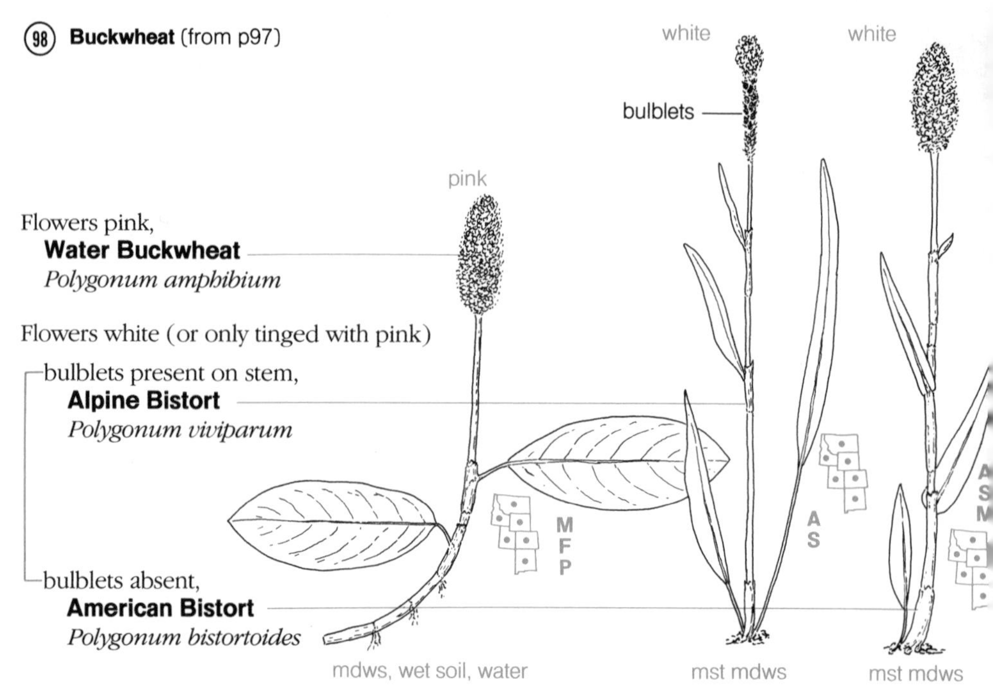
white
white
bulblets
pink
M
F
P
A
S
mdws, wet soil, water
mst mdws
mst mdws

PURSLANE FAMILY *(Portulacaceae)* Regular flowers with four to eight separate petals, two sepals (except *Lewisia rediviva*). Ovary superior, stamens opposite petals. Leaves simple.

S
M
F

MN pink

Many petals,
Bitterroot
Lewisia rediviva

grvl mdws & slps

Four to eight petals; leaves

— basal,
Pigmy Bitterroot
Lewisia pygmaea

pink

A S M

mst mdws & slps

— single pair on stem,
Springbeauty
Claytonia lanceolata

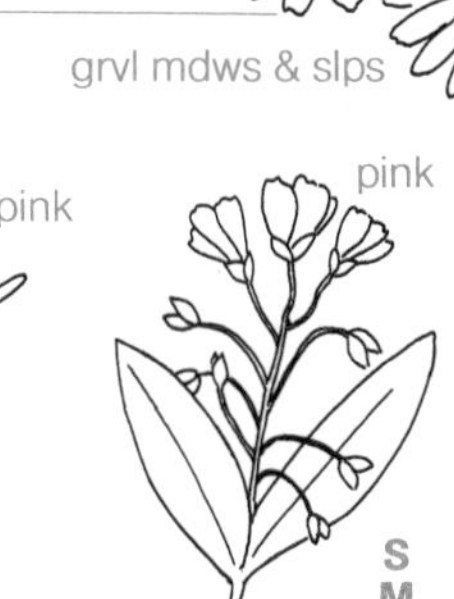

pink

S M F

mdws, slps, wds

— several pairs on stem,
Water Springbeauty
Montia chamissoi

white or pink

M F

wet soil

PRIMROSE FAMILY *(Primulaceae)* Flowers regular with five united petals, superior ovary. Stamens opposite petals. Leaves simple, mostly basal.

Flowers white, tiny,
Rock Primrose
Androsace septentrionalis

Flowers pink to lavender, and

- pointed like a dart,
  Shooting Star
  Dodecatheon pulchellum
- not pointed; plant is
  - mat forming,
    Rocky Mountain Douglasia
    Douglasia montana
  - not as above,
    Parry Primrose
    Primula parryi

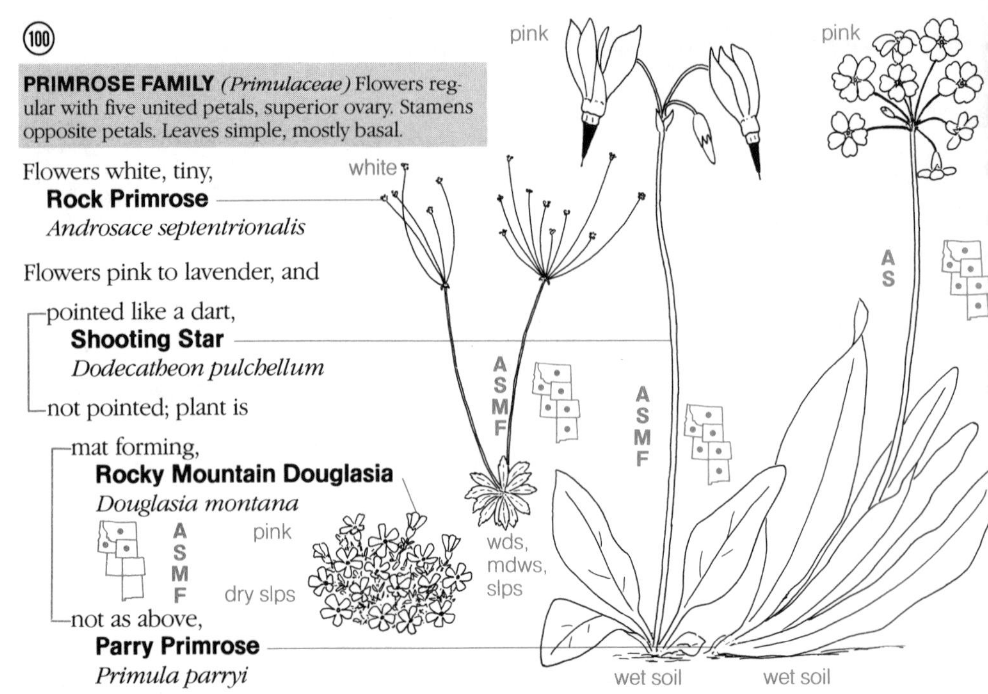

white
ASMF
wds, mdws, slps
pink
ASMF
wet soil
pink
AS
wet soil
ASMF
pink
dry slps

WINTERGREEN FAMILY *(Pyrolaceae)* Herbs with or without chlorophyll. Flowers usually regular with four or five petals; ovary superior. Usually growing in forests.

Plant green, next page.

Plant not green (lacks chlorophyll); petals are

- united,
  Pinedrops
  Pterospora andromedea
- separate,
  Pinesap
  Monotropa hypopitys

M. uniflora (Indian Pipe), illus.,plant white or pinkish, flowers one per stalk.

white
S
M
F
mst wds

whitish
or reddish
yellowish
M
F
S
M
F
wds
wds

Wintergreen (from p101)

Flowers solitary,

One-flowered Wintergreen
Moneses uniflora

Flowers not solitary; leaves
- whorled,
  Pipsissewa
  Chimaphila umbellata
- basal,
  Pyrola
  Pyrola sp.

P. asarifolia (Bog Pyrola), illus.; *P. chlorantha* (Green Pyrola), flowers greenish white, styles long, curved down; *P. minor* (Least Pyrola), flowers white to pinkish, styles short, straight; *P. secunda* (One-sided Pyrola), flowers greenish white on one side of the stem.

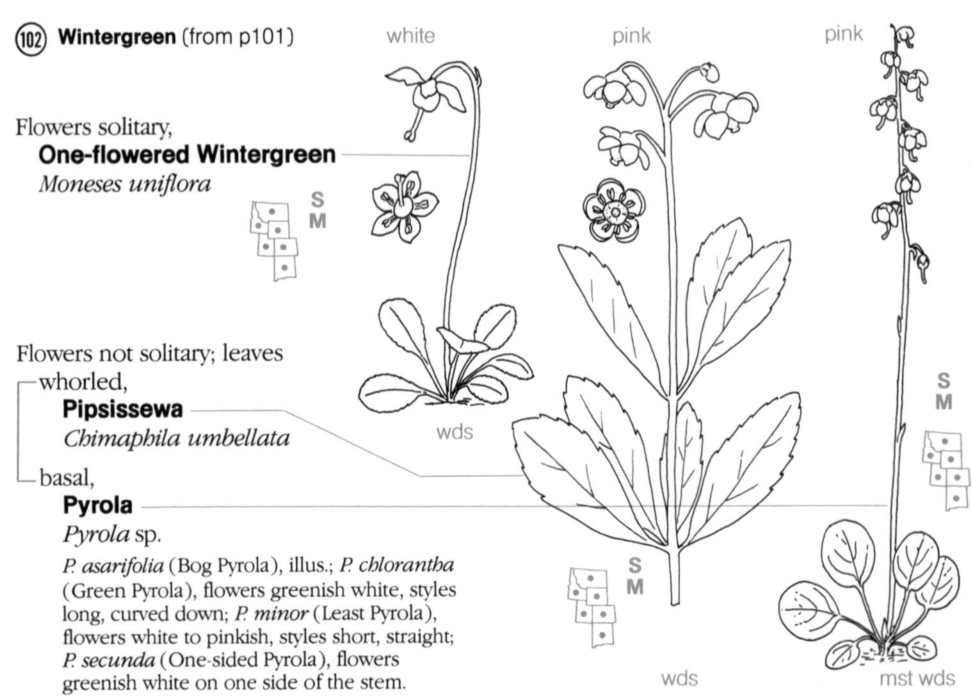
white
pink
pink
S
M
wds
S
M
S
M
wds
mst wds

BUTTERCUP FAMILY *(Ranunculaceae)* Flowers mostly regular with none to many petals. Sepals often petal-like when petals are absent. Many stamens, three to many pistils. Leaves are often lobed or divided.

Plant a vine,

Yellow Clematis

Clematis orientale

C. columbiana, flowers blue-violet.

Plant not a vine; flowers are

- regular, next page.
- irregular, spurred,

  Larkspur

  Delphinium sp.

  D. barbeyi (Subalpine Larkspur), plant tall, stems hairy; *D. geyeri,* flowers bright blue, foothills; *D. nuttallianum,* illus., flowers dark blue, plant small; *D. occidentale* (Tall Larkspur), plant tall, stem not hairy; *D. virescens* (Plains Larkspur), flowers white to pale blue.
- irregular, unspurred,

  American Monkshood

  Aconitum columbianum

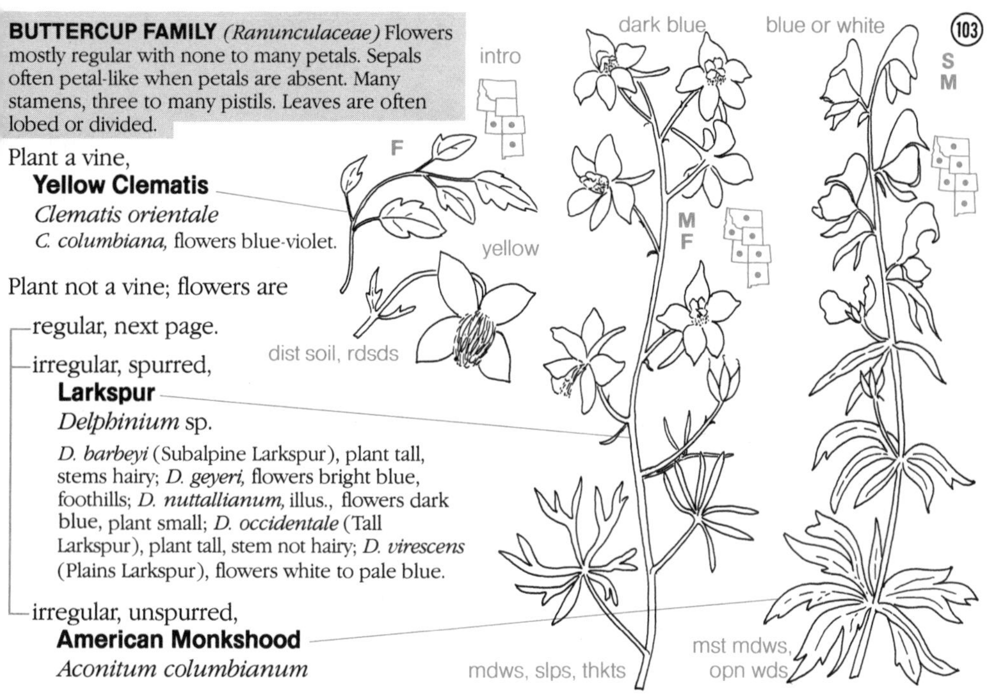
intro
F
yellow
dist soil, rdsds
dark blue
M
F
mdws, slps, thkts
blue or white
S
M
mst mdws,
opn wds

(104) **Buttercup** (from p103)

Spurs present,

Colorado Blue Columbine

Aquilegia caerulea

A. chrysantha (Golden Columbine), *A. elegantula* (Rocky Mountain Red Columbine), *A. flavescens* (Northern Yellow Columbine).

Spurs absent; flowers are

- purple, lavender-blue or greenish, next page.
- white, cream, or pale yellow (sometimes blue/purple tinged), p106.
- pink or red,

  Red Anemone

  Anemone multifida ssp. *globosa*
- bright yellow; upper petal surface shiny,

  Buttercup

  Ranunculus sp.

  R. alismaefolius; R. cymbalaria, illus.; *R. gmelinii,* aquatic; *R. glaberrimus;* others.

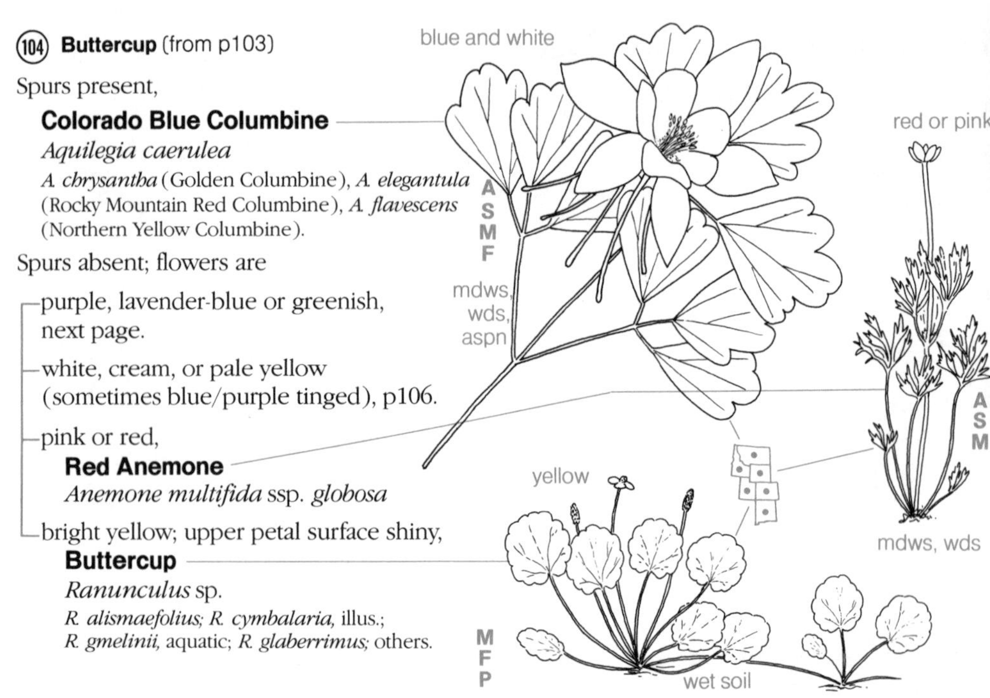
blue and white
A
S
M
F
mdws,
wds,
aspn
red or pink
A
S
M
mdws, wds
yellow
M
F
P
wet soil

Buttercup (from p104)

Flowers small, inconspicuous,
Meadowrue
Thalictrum sp.
T. dasycarpum; T. fendleri, illus.;
T. occidentale; T. sparsiflorum; others.

Flowers large, conspicuous and

- nodding,
  Sugar Bowls
  Clematis hirsutissima
- erect,
  Pasque Flower
  Pulsatilla patens ssp. *multifida*

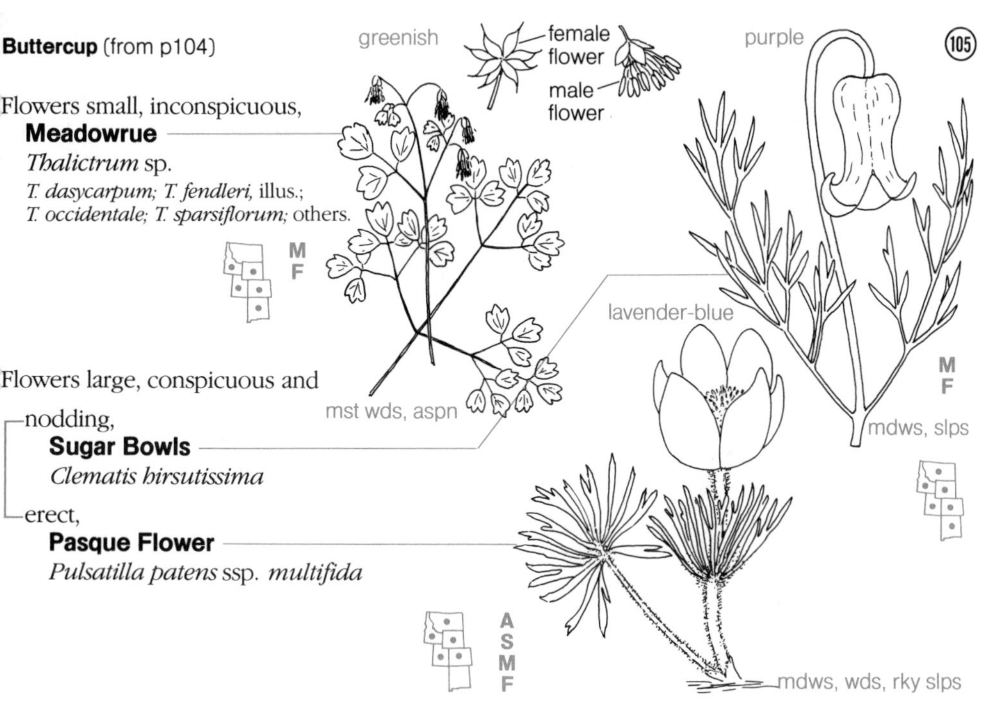
greenish
female flower
male flower
M
F
mst wds, aspn
purple
lavender-blue
M
F
mdws, slps
A
S
M
F
mdws, wds, rky slps

(106) **Buttercup** (from p104)

Plant aquatic,

Water Crowfoot
Ranunculus aquatilis

Plant terrestrial; flowers are

- fewer than five per stem, next page.
- more than five, leaves are
  - palmately lobed or parted,
    False Bugbane
    Trautvetteria caroliniensis
  - pinnately compound,
    Baneberry
    Actaea rubra ssp. *arguta*

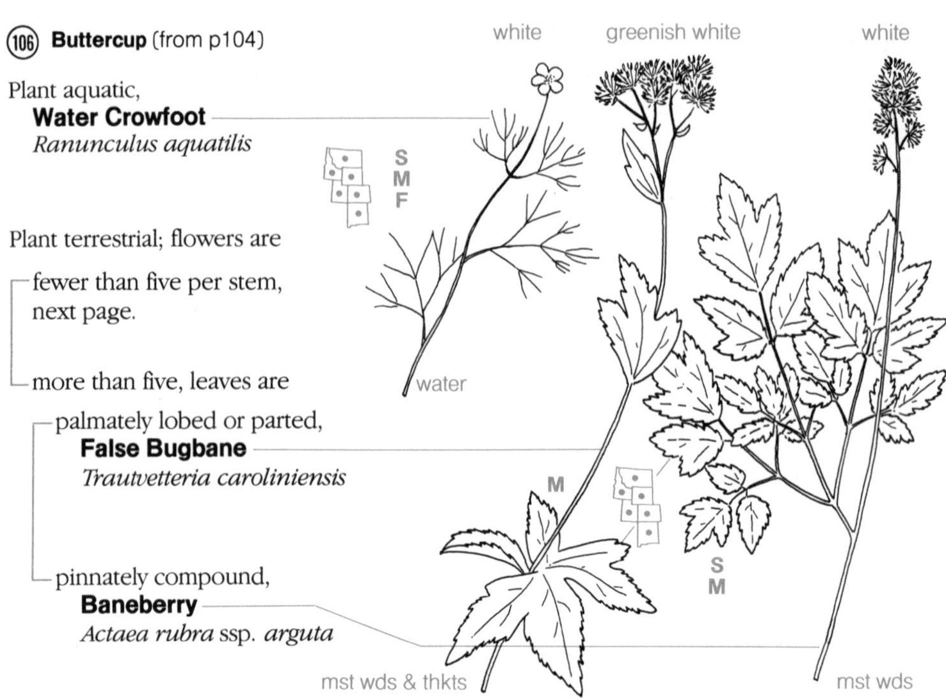
white
greenish white
white
S
M
F
water
M
S
M
mst wds & thkts
mst wds

Buttercup (from p106)

Plant hairy; petals are

—about 1in long,

Western Pasque Flower

Pulsatilla occidentalis

—smaller,

Windflower

Anemone sp.

A. canadensis (Meadow Anemone), illus.; *A. cylindrica* (Thimbleweed), receptacle elongate; *A. narcissiflora,* flowers umbellate, three or more.

Plant not hairy; leaves are

—mostly basal,

Marsh Marigold

Caltha leptosepala

—present on stem,

Globeflower

Trollius laxus var. *albiflorus*

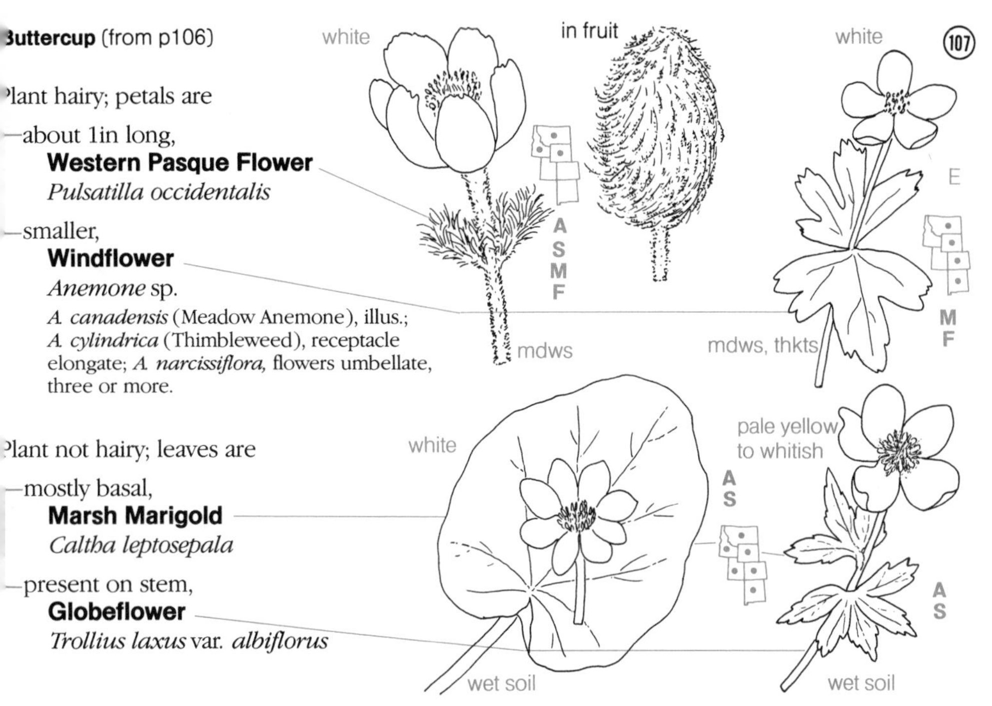
white
in fruit
white
A
S
M
F
mdws
E
M
F
mdws, thkts
white
pale yellow
to whitish
A
S
A
S
wet soil
wet soil

ROSE FAMILY *(Rosaceae)* Regular flowers with five separate petals, five sepals which appear united at base, usually many stamens and pistils in herbaceous plants. Petals, sepals and stamens set on the rim of a floral cup. Leaves simple or compound, usually with stipules.

Flowers white, next page.

Flowers yellow or greenish, p110.

Flowers pink to purplish, usually nodding; leaves

- finely divided,
  Pink Plumes
  Geum triflorum
- not finely divided,
  Purple Avens
  Geum rivale

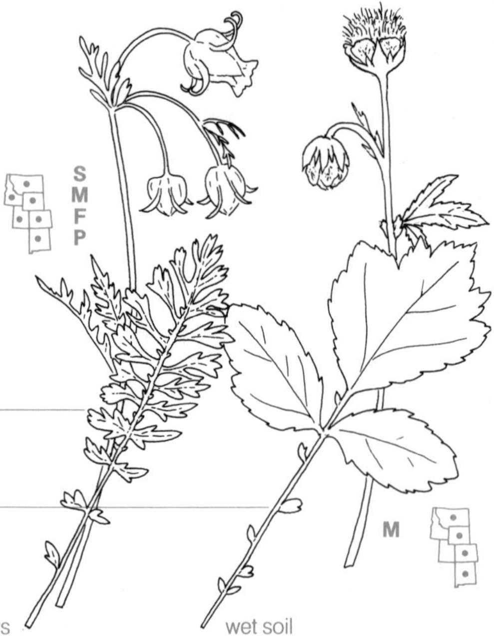

reddish pink
purplish
S
M
F
P
M
mdws
wet soil

Leaflets narrow,
Nuttall Chamaerhodos
Chamaerhodos erecta ssp. *nuttallii*

Leaflets wide and
three,
Wild Strawberry
Fragaria virginiana var. *glauca*

more than three,
Sticky Cinquefoil
Potentilla arguta

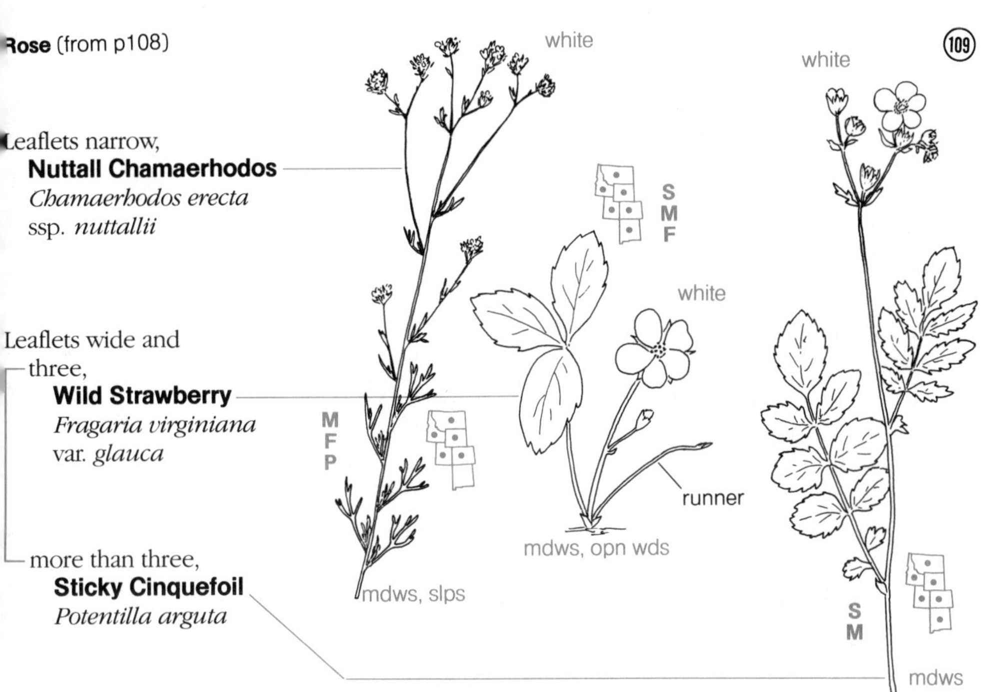
white
MFP
mdws, slps
white
SMF
runner
mdws, opn wds
white
SM
mdws

Rose (from p108)

Fruit a bur; plant over 1ft tall; inflorescence is

- a raceme,
  Agrimony
  Agrimonia striata
- branched,
  Bur Avens
  Geum macrophyllum

Fruit not a bur; plant usually shorter; leaves are

- pinnately compound, next page.
- palmately compound; flowers are
  - inconspicuous; leaflets three,
    Sibbaldia
    Sibbaldia procumbens
  - conspicuous,
    Potentilla, Cinquefoil
    Potentilla sp.
    P. diversifolia (Blueleaf Cinquefoil), illus.;
    P. gracilis (Goldcup Potentilla); others.

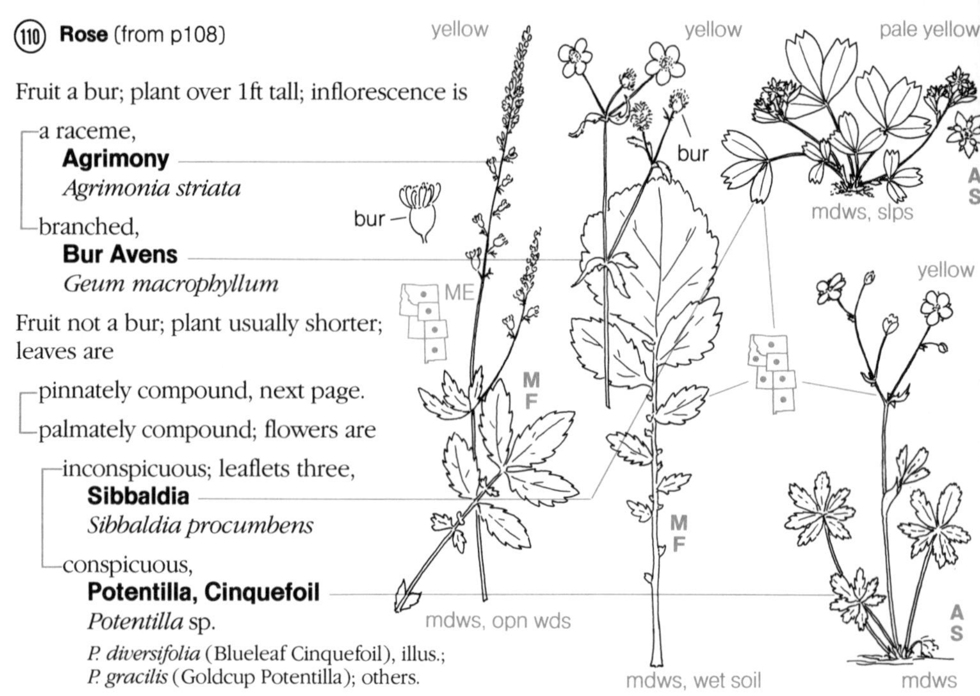
yellow
bur
ME
M F
mdws, opn wds
yellow
bur
M F
mdws, wet soil
pale yellow
A S
mdws, slps
yellow
A S
mdws

Plant of upper subalpine, alpine zones, with dark green, mostly basal leaves; style remains on mature fruit,
Alpine Avens
Geum rossii

Plant not as above in all characteristics,
Potentilla, Cinquefoil
Potentilla sp.
P. fissa (Leafy Cinquefoil), illus., stems with spreading hairs; *P. anserina* (Silverweed), runners; *P. hippiana* (Silvery Potentilla), leaflets entirely white hairy; others.

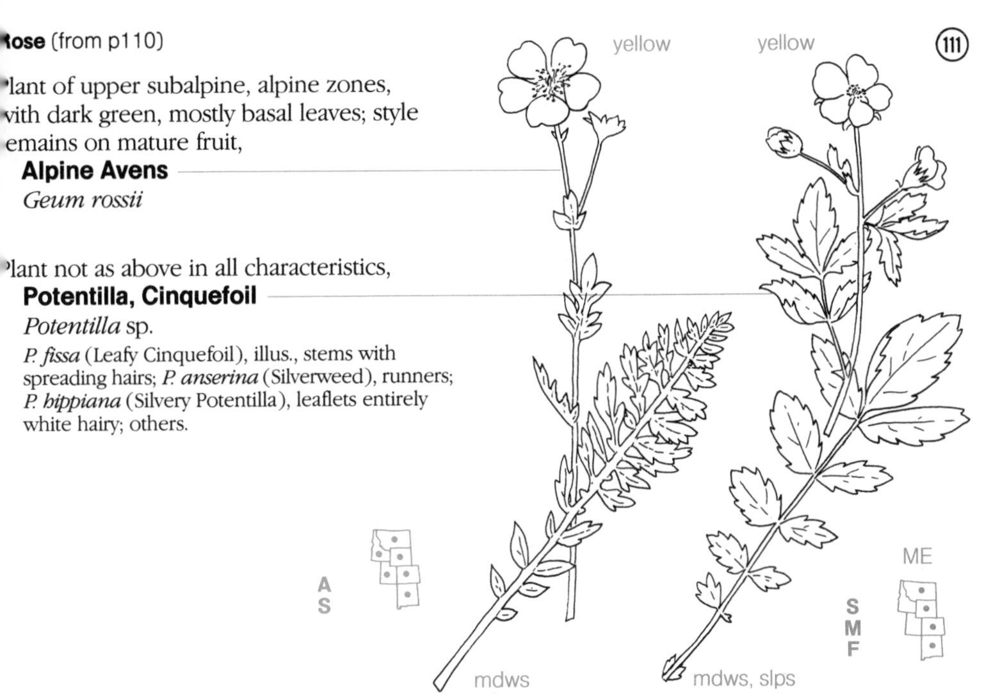
yellow
yellow
A
S
mdws
mdws, slps
ME
S
M
F

MADDER FAMILY *(Rubiaceae)* Tiny regular flowers with four united petals, inferior ovary which develops into a two-lobed fruit. Stem square with opposite or whorled simple entire leaves.

Northern Bedstraw

Galium boreale

G. trifidum (Small Bedstraw), leaves narrow; *G. triflorum* (Fragrant Bedstraw), leaves wide. Both with inconspicuous flowers.

S
M
F

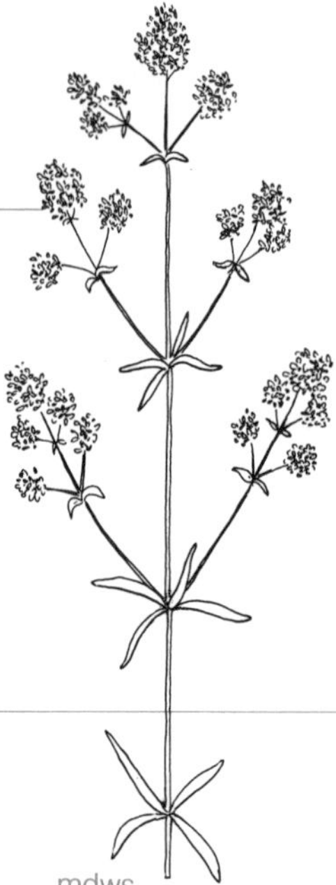

white

mdws

SANDALWOOD FAMILY *(Santalaceae)* Small hairless perennial plants with no petals but four or five white, greenish or pinkish petal-like sepals. Ovary inferior. Leaves simple. Partially parasitic.

Bastard Toadflax

Comandra umbellata

white, greenish or pinkish

dry mdws & slps

F
P

AXIFRAGE FAMILY *(Saxifragaceae)* Regular
owers with five petals, five or ten stamens, one pistil
hich is commonly two-horned. Leaves often en-
ely basal. Leaves usually palmately veined or lobed.

lant matted, moss-like; petals spotted,
Dotted Saxifrage
Saxifraga bronchialis

lant not as above; stem has

–no leaves, next page.

–a single leaf,
Parnassia
Parnassia sp.
P. fimbriata (Fringed Parnassia), illus., leaf near middle of stem; *P. parviflora* (Small-flowered Parnassia), leaf below middle of stem.

–more than one leaf,
Woodland Star
Lithophragma sp.
L. glabrum, illus., flowers pink, stem reddish with bulblets; *P. parviflorum,* flowers white or pinkish, stem green with no bulblets.

white
white
pink
A
S
M
A
S
M
M
dry wds, rky slps
wet soil
opn wds

(114) **Saxifrage** (from p113)

Flowers in congested, ball-like cluster (s),

Snowball Saxifrage
Saxifraga rhomboidea

Flowers in open panicle,

Brook Saxifrage
Saxifraga odontoloma

Flowers in raceme or spike; petals are

- pinnately fringed,
  Bishops Cap
  Mitella pentandra
- three-lobed,
  Small-flower Miterwort
  Mitella stauropetala
- not as above,
  Alumroot
  Heuchera sp.
  H. bracteata (Bracted Alumroot), illus., stamens protruding, leaf teeth pointed; *H. parviflora* (Common Alumroot), stamens included, leaf teeth rounded.

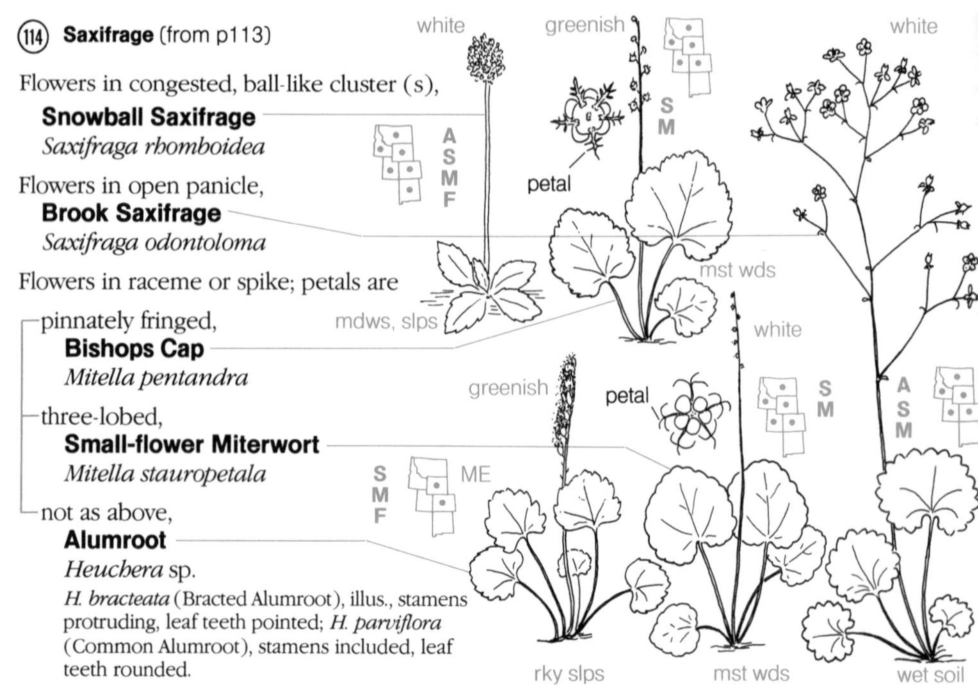
white
A
S
M
F
mdws, slps
greenish
petal
S
M
mst wds
white
A
S
M
wet soil
greenish
S
M
F
ME
rky slps
petal
white
S
M
mst wds

FIGWORT FAMILY *(Scrophulariaceae)* Irregular flowers with four or five united petals. Ovary superior.

Leaves alternate or basal, p117.

Leaves opposite; petals are

- blue, purplish or lavender to whitish, next page.
- reddish brown, **Bunny-in-the-grass** *Scrophularia lanceolata*
- yellow, **Yellow Monkeyflower** *Mimulus guttatus*
  M. floribundus, similar.
- pink to red; a plant of
  - wet areas, **Red Monkeyflower** *Mimulus lewisii*
  - dry areas, **Scarlet Penstemon** *Penstemon barbatus*
    P. eatonii (Firecracker Penstemon), slightly two-lipped flowers, southern Rockies.

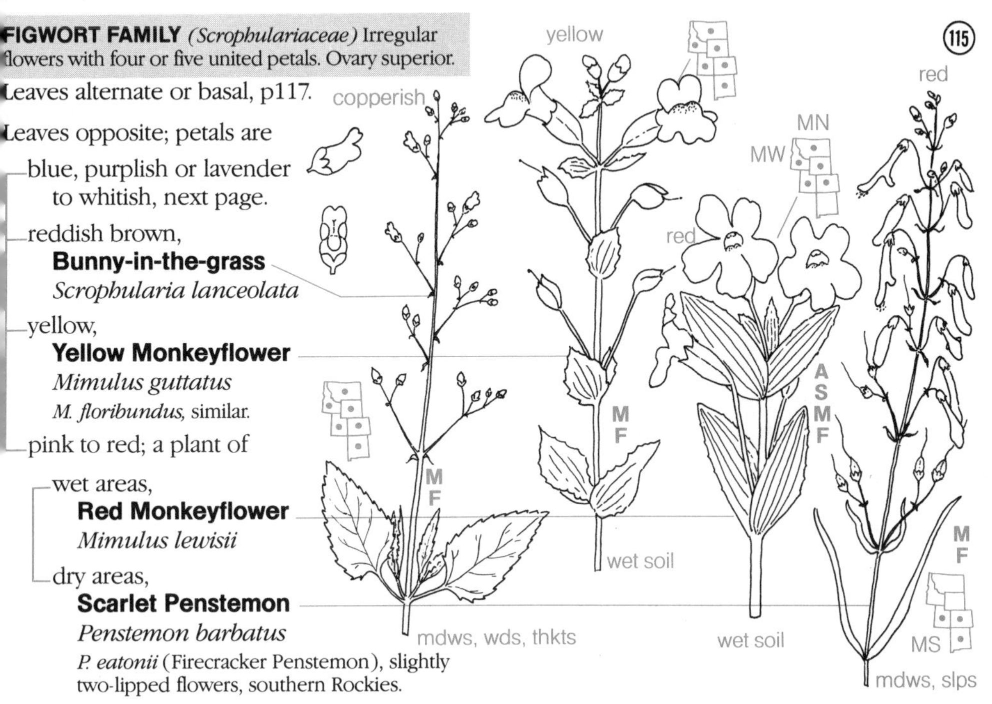
copperish
M
F
mdws, wds, thkts
yellow
M
F
wet soil
red
MN
MW
A
S
M
F
wet soil
red
M
F
MS
mdws, slps

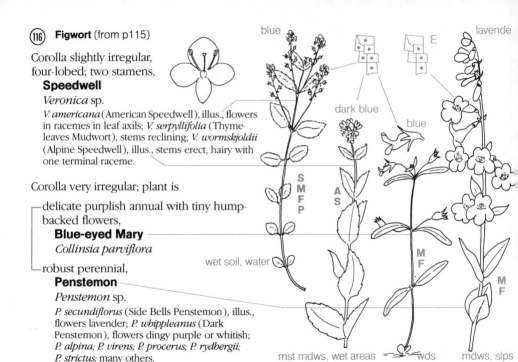

(116) **Figwort** (from p115)

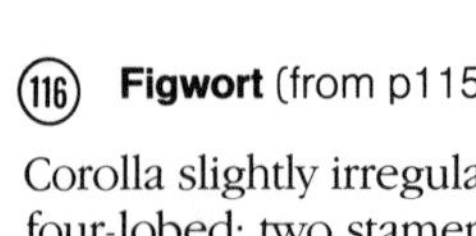

Corolla slightly irregular, four-lobed; two stamens,

Speedwell

Veronica sp.

V. americana (American Speedwell), illus., flowers in racemes in leaf axils; *V. serpyllifolia* (Thyme-leaves Mudwort), stems reclining; *V. wormskjoldii* (Alpine Speedwell), illus., stems erect, hairy with one terminal raceme.

Corolla very irregular; plant is

- delicate purplish annual with tiny hump-backed flowers,

  Blue-eyed Mary

  Collinsia parviflora

- robust perennial,

  Penstemon

  Penstemon sp.

  P. secundiflorus (Side Bells Penstemon), illus., flowers lavender; *P. whippleanus* (Dark Penstemon), flowers dingy purple or whitish; *P. alpina; P. virens; P. procerus; P. rydbergii; P. strictus;* many others.

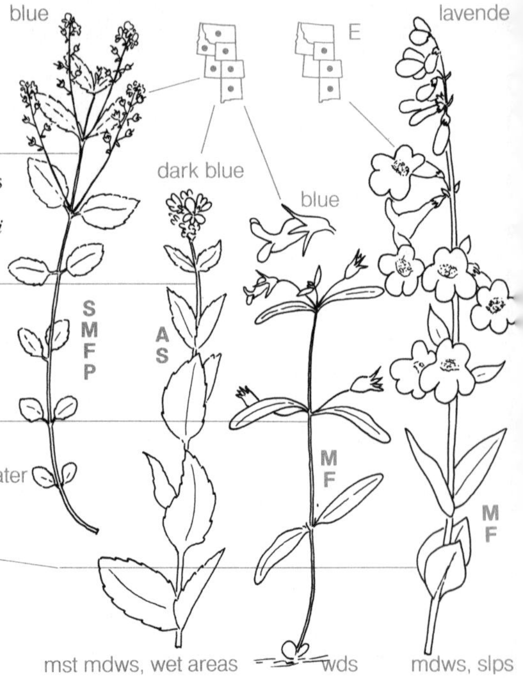

blue

SMFP

wet soil, water

dark blue

AS

mst mdws, wet areas

blue

MF

wds

E

lavende

MF

mdws, slps

Figwort (from p115)

Plant densely woolly, 2-5ft tall,
Woolly Mullein
Verbascum thapsus

Plant not as above; stamens

extend beyond petals,
Kittentail
Besseya plantaginea

not as above; corolla is

mostly greenish, hidden by colored calyx and bracts,
Paintbrush
Castilleja sp.

C. integra, illus.; *C. chromosa,* red, orange-red; *C. linariifolia,* red; *C. miniata,* red; *C. occidentalis,* yellow; *C. rhexifolia,* pink to purple; *C. sulphurea,* yellow; others.

not as above, next page.

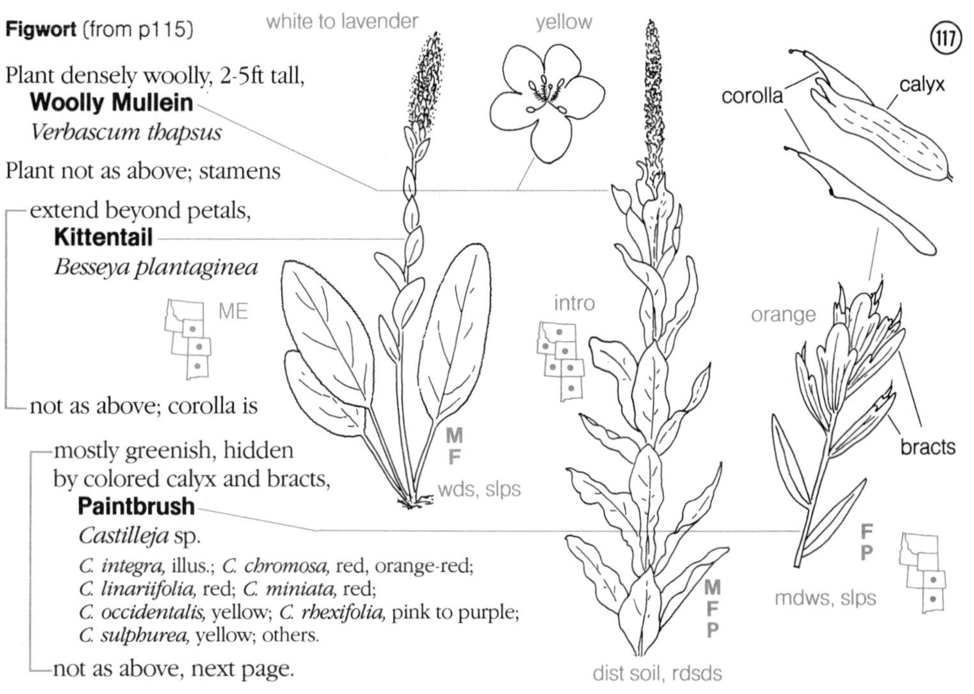
white to lavender
ME
M
F
wds, slps
yellow
intro
M
F
P
dist soil, rdsds
corolla
calyx
orange
bracts
F
P
mdws, slps

(118) **Figwort** (from p117)

Leaves simple, entire or with a few lobes; spur is

- present,
  Toadflax *Linaria* sp.
  L. genistifolia ssp. *dalmatica,* leaves broad; *L. vulgaris* (Butter-and-eggs), illus., leaves narrow.
- absent,
  Owlclover *Orthocarpus luteus*

Leaves compound, or simple with many lobes or teeth; flowers are

- elephant-head shaped,
  Little Red Elephant
  Pedicularis groenlandica
- not as above,
  Lousewort *Pedicularis* sp.
  P. bracteosa ssp. *paysoniana* (Bracted Lousewort), illus.; *P. crenulata* (Purple Lousewort), flowers purple, leaves simple; *P. procera,* flowers greenish or yellowish with red streaks; *P. racemosa* (Curled Lousewort), flowers cream colored, leaves simple.

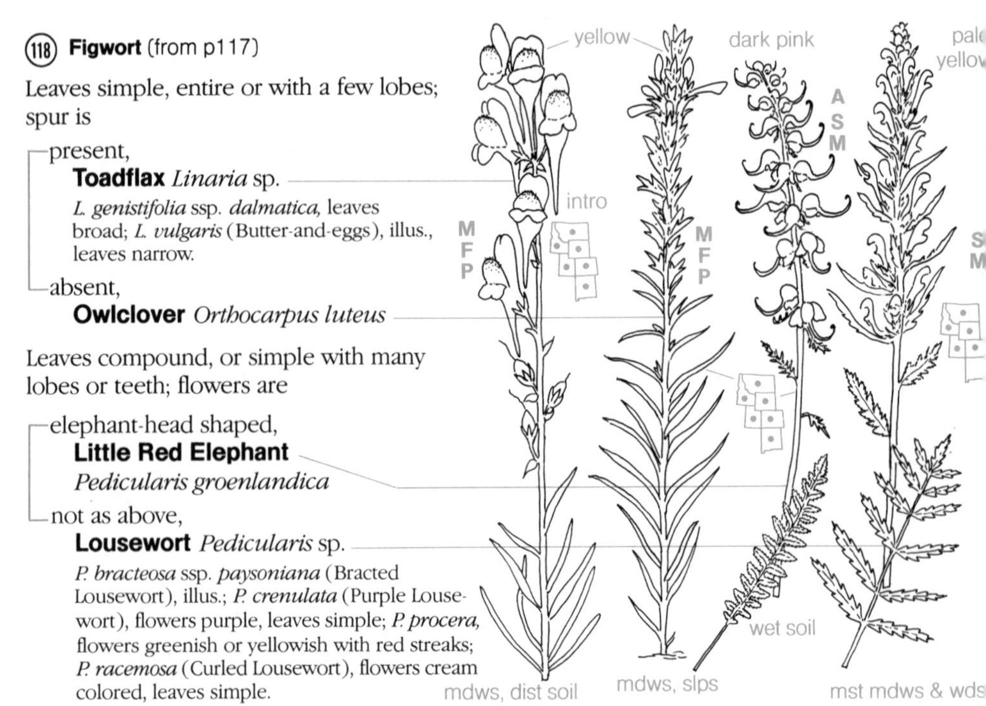
yellow
dark pink
intro
M F P
M F P
A S M
wet soil
mdws, dist soil
mdws, slps
mst mdws & wds

VALERIAN FAMILY *(Valerianaceae)* Small somewhat irregular flowers with five united petals, sepals that become plume-like in fruit, three stamens, inferior ovary. Leaves opposite.

Valerian

Valeriana sp.

V. edule, illus., flowers in open panicle; *V. capitata,* flowers in dense cluster.

VERBENA FAMILY *(Verbenaceae)* Somewhat irregular flowers with united petals. Leaves opposite.

Wild Verbena

Verbena ambrosifolia

V. bracteata (Bracted Vervain), flowers tiny.

VIOLET FAMILY *(Violaceae)* Irregular flowers with five separate petals. Leaves simple, alternate or basal.

Violet

Viola sp.

V. nuttallii, flowers yellow; *V. canadensis,* flowers white; *V. adunca,* illus.; others.

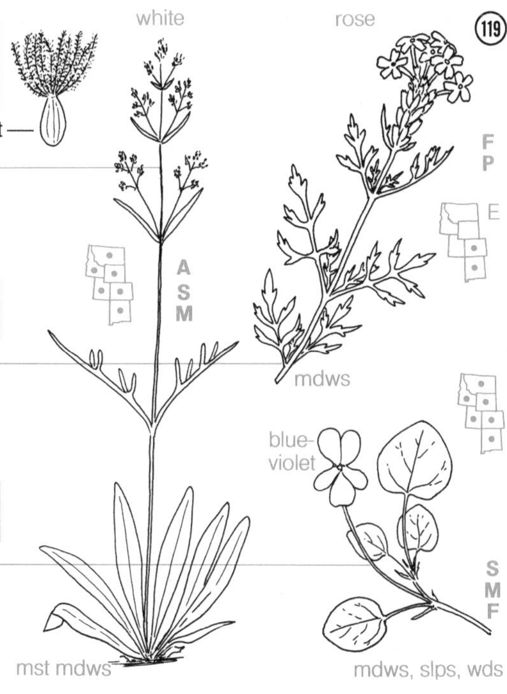
white
fruit
A
S
M
mst mdws
rose
F
P
E
mdws
blue-
violet
S
M
F
mdws, slps, wds

INDEX

other books like this one, and what they identify:

for eastern North America

- **FLOWER FINDER**—spring wildflowers and flower families
- **TREE FINDER**—all native and introduced trees
- **WINTER TREE FINDER**—leafless winter trees
- **FERN FINDER**—native northeastern and midwestern ferns
- **TRACK FINDER**—tracks and footprints of mammals
- **BERRY FINDER**—native plants with fleshy fruits
- **LIFE ON INTERTIDAL ROCKS**—intertidal plants and animals
- **WINTER WEED FINDER**—dry plant structures in winter
- **BIRD FINDER**—some common birds and how they live

for Pacific coast states

- **PACIFIC COAST TREE FINDER**—native trees, Sitka to San Diego
- **PACIFIC COAST BIRD FINDER**—some common birds, how they live
- **PACIFIC COAST BERRY FINDER**—native plants with fleshy fruits
- **PACIFIC COAST FERN FINDER**—native ferns and fern relatives
- **REDWOOD REGION FLOWER FINDER**—wildflowers and families
- **SIERRA FLOWER FINDER**—wildflowers of the Sierra Nevada
- **PACIFIC INTERTIDAL LIFE**—organisms of pools, rocks and reefs
- **MAMMAL FINDER**—mammals, their tracks, other signs
- **PACIFIC COAST FISH**—marine fish, Alaska to Mexico

for Rocky Mt. and desert states

- **DESERT TREE FINDER**—desert trees of CA, AZ, NM
- **ROCKY MOUNTAIN TREE FINDER**—native Rocky Mountain trees
- **ROCKY MOUNTAIN FLOWER FINDER**—wildflowers below tree line

for a catalog write **NATURE STUDY GUILD, box 972, Berkeley, California 94701**